THE FOUR BOOKS

THE BASIC TEACHINGS OF THE
LATER CONFUCIAN TRADITION

D1637019

THE FOUR BOOKS

THE BASIC TEACHINGS OF THE
LATER CONFUCIAN TRADITION

Translations, with Introduction
and Commentary, by

DANIEL K. GARDNER

Hackett Publishing Company, Inc.
Indianapolis/Cambridge

20   19   18   17   16   3   4   5   6   7   8

For further information, please address:

Hackett Publishing Company, Inc.
P.O. Box 44937
Indianapolis, IN 46244-0937

www.hackettpublishing.com

Cover design by Abigail Coyle
Text design by Carrie Wagner

Library of Congress Cataloging-in-Publication Data
Si shu. English.
    Four books: the basic teachings of the later Confucian tradition / translated
with introduction and commentary by Daniel K. Gardner.
        p.   cm.
    Includes index.
    ISBN 978-0-87220-826-1 (pbk.)
    ISBN 978-0-87220-827-8
    1. Si shu.   I. Gardner, Daniel K., 1950-   II. Title.   III. Title: Basic
teachings of the later Confucian tradition.
    PL2463.Z6S75 2007
    181′.112—dc22
                                                              2006038036

To my sister Cindy and her family—
Bob, Andrew, Madeleine, and Elizabeth

CONTENTS

Acknowledgments ix

Illustrations xi

Introduction: The Four Books in Chinese Society xiii

The *Great Learning* 3

The *Analects* 11

The *Mencius* 53

Maintaining Perfect Balance 107

Conclusion: Interpreting the Four Books 131

Works Cited 148

Suggested Readings 151

Glossary/Index of Important Names and Terms 152

ACKNOWLEDGMENTS

This book is, to a large extent, the product of years of teaching undergraduates about China. In offering courses on later Chinese history and thought, I have found that, although standard textbooks and monographs emphasize the importance of the Confucian canon, and especially of the Four Books—in education, the civil service system, the "Confucian orthodoxy," and the maintenance of social norms—few explain in detail what the Four Books taught or how the Chinese of the later imperial period (1200–1900) studied these texts and assimilated their values. This one-volume introduction to the Four Books is designed, out of some frustration, to fill this gap, and thus indirectly owes much to my students and courses. I have chosen here what I believe to be the most meaningful and interesting passages from each of these texts, translated them, and explained them as they were read by Zhu Xi (1130–1200), the Song philosopher whose commentaries on these texts provided the standard interpretation of them in China, and indeed, all of East Asia, for the next seven hundred years. The use of interlinear commentary in this study is intended to show the English reader how the Chinese have typically read and understood the Four Books since the Song dynasty (960–1279).

Cynthia Brokaw, as ever, has given generously of her time to read drafts of the book and to talk through myriad problems that arose as I worked through the manuscript. She has my heartfelt thanks. She is the sounding board that has made this project better—and far more pleasurable for me—than it would have been otherwise. Readers will never know the gratitude they too owe her. I owe a thanks, too, to Marilyn Rhie, a generous colleague of many years, for helping me to select the Shen Zhou painting that graces the cover.

Deborah Wilkes at Hackett Publishing has been the ideal editor. She took an uncommon interest in the project from beginning to end, encouraging me throughout and keeping me to task. Her editorial eye was sharp, her touch gentle. The questions she raised always provoked or clarified.

Finally, Claudia and Jeremy, I am confident that you need never read these acknowledgments to know how much you mean to me.

ILLUSTRATIONS

FIG. 1 A Village School
xii

FIG. 2 Backing the Book
xii

FIG. 3 Examination Hall
xvi

FIG. 4 Individual Examination Cells
xvi

FIG. 5 Celebrating a Winner of the Jinshi degee
xvii

FIG. 6 Classical Text
xxviii

Fig. 1 A Village School, by Zhang Hong, dated 1649. From James Cahill, *The Restless Landscape: Chinese Painting of the Late Ming Period* (Berkeley: Chinese Art Museum, 1971).

Fig. 2 Backing the Book. From Justus Doolittle, *Social Life of the Chinese: With Some Account of Their Religious, Governmental, Educational and Business Customs and Opinions.* (New York: Harper & Bros., 1867).

INTRODUCTION

THE FOUR BOOKS IN
CHINESE SOCIETY

You are a Chinese boy aged seven, born into a family intent on your receiving an education. The year could be any between 1200 and 1900. Your family, if an especially prosperous one, may have engaged a private tutor to teach you at home, perhaps in an elegant study overlooking a tranquil garden with a small pond. More likely, however, your family has but meager resources and has arranged for you to go to the local village school. The school, no larger than a room or two, is dingy and cramped, run by a teacher whose youthful hope of becoming an official has died (Fig. 1). Teaching, for him, is little more than a means of survival. His pay is limited, as is his dedication.

But whether your education takes place in idyllic surroundings with a private tutor or in a squalid schoolroom with a teacher eking out a livelihood, the texts at the center of your studies will be the same: the Four Books. For at least the next eight years—assuming you continue with your education—you will devote yourself to learning the *Great Learning*, the *Analects*, the *Mencius*, and *Maintaining Perfect Balance*. The process will be arduous and not necessarily intellectually challenging or stimulating. Most of your time will be spent in rote memorization, in the exercise of "backing the book." You will approach the teacher's desk, and with your back to him you will recite aloud, from memory, the line or lines he has asked you to prepare from the book he holds in his hands (Fig. 2). If your recitation is flawless, you will return to your desk and begin work on the next line in the text; forget a word or confuse word order and, with the thwack of a bamboo rod, you will be ordered back to your seat to continue with the memorization efforts. This learning regimen ensures that by the time you are fifteen you will "know" the Four Books; you will be capable of reciting each of them front to back, line by line, without error.

But your knowledge and capability will go further still. You will be able to recite line by line the extensive interlinear commentary prepared for each by the great *Daoxue* 道學 (lit., "school of the Way"; commonly translated as Neo-Confucianism) scholar of the Song dynasty, Zhu Xi 朱熹 (1130–1200). It is his commentary that the political and intellectual elite agree best captures the significance of the Four Books, and so it is his commentary that will appear in your editions of the books and will serve as the basis of your understanding of them. When asked by a teacher to explain the meaning of a passage in the Four Books, your explanation will be expected to echo that of Zhu Xi.

Come age fifteen, if your talent is sufficient and if your family's financial resources hold out, you will likely continue with your education, focusing your aim on the civil service examinations—a series of examinations in which success in the first stage, at the district level, entitles one to move on to the examination in the provincial capital; success there, in turn, qualifies one to sit for a set of examinations at the imperial capital, the last one presided over by the emperor himself. The competition in these exams, even at the local level, is fierce, but success in them seems to justify the investment of sweat and resources, both yours and your family's. What is required to advance successfully from the district exam to the provincial exam, and then from the provincial exam to the metropolitan exam, is precisely what has brought you acclaim from teachers and family members since the age of seven: knowledge of the Four Books and their commentaries (Figs. 3 and 4).

Passing the final stage of the examinations at the capital and acquiring the *jinshi* 進士 ("presented-scholar") degree all but guarantee you will achieve high official position and win status, reputation, and influence for your family for years to come. The day the results of the examination are announced, your name will be written on a placard and posted in the capital; you will be paraded around on a horse or litter decorated in gay red ribbons; and imperial

runners will be sent from the capital to your local village to proclaim to one and all the spectacular success of one of its native sons
(Fig. 5). Because you are a winner of the *jinshi* degree, prominent
families will now compete to marry their daughters to you; rich
merchants will be eager to lend you and your relatives money at
highly favorable terms, perhaps even interest free; and local gentry
will send gifts of livestock, books, food, and even cash in celebration
of your great achievement.

   In short, no texts had greater presence or power in later imperial
China than the Four Books. Just as knowledge of the Bible among
literate people was assumed in Europe in medieval and early modern
times, so was knowledge of the Four Books assumed in China.
These books were considered sacred texts, for they were the
direct words and teachings of the great sages of antiquity, men
whose exemplary wisdom and virtue served as an eternal model
for the ages. Similarly—as the Bible in the West—passages, paragraphs, lines, and terms from these books became part of the *lingua
franca* in China, used referentially in speech and writing by literati
who could be confident that there existed a shared cultural
inheritance.

   If these Four Books were endowed with so much power, how
had that come to be? Since the second century BCE, the intellectual and political elite had singled out certain texts within the
tradition as being especially worthwhile, especially significant.
These texts they called *jing* 經, conventionally translated as "classic"
or "canon." The first texts to be so designated, in the Early Han
(206 BCE–9 CE), were known collectively as the *wujing* 五經, or Five
Classics:

> The *CLASSIC OF CHANGES*, a text that in its earliest portions is
> a divination manual enabling users to foretell change in the uni-
> verse and, based on such knowledge, to act prudently; later por-
> tions of the text are treatises elaborating on the early cosmological
> views of the Chinese.
>
> The *BOOK OF ODES*, a compilation of over three hundred odes
> made roughly in the middle of the first millennium BCE that

Fig. 3   Examination Hall, Nanjing. From Arthur Judson Brown, *The Chinese Revolution*. (Student Volunteer Movement: New York, 1912).

Fig. 4   Individual Examination Cells, Nanjing. From Etienne Zi, *Pratique des examens littéraires* (Shanghai: Imprimerie de la Mission Catholique, 1894).

Fig. 5   Celebrating a Winner of the *Jinshi* degree. From Ming Zhuanyuan, edited by Gu Dingchen. (Beijing: Zhongguo Shudian, 1999).

includes folk songs, festive ballads, odes of lament, court poetry, and dynastic hymns.

The **BOOK OF HISTORY**, a collection of documents, speeches, and pronouncements all on the general theme of governance, the earliest of which purports to deal with the reign of the legendary sage-king Yao.

The **BOOK OF RITES**, a compendium of rituals and rules of etiquette, the mastery of which is necessary for the maintenance of a harmonious society.

The **SPRING AND AUTUMN ANNALS**, a chronicle of events occurring in or affecting the state of Lu, the native state of Confucius, during the period from 722 to 481 BCE.

These Five Classics constituted the curriculum in the newly established (124 BCE) Imperial Academy; students who at the end of the year demonstrated mastery in one or more of these texts and familiarity with the commentaries that had grown up around them would become expectant officials, filling positions in the bureaucracy as they became vacant.

From the Han period through the early years of the Song (960–1279), the canon grew from the foundational five to thirteen. Many of the additional texts marked for inclusion in the canon were just commentaries or glosses on the original five: the *Zuo Tradition* (which was incorporated into the *Sung su Autumn Annals*), the *Gongyang Tradition*, and the *Guliang Tradition* were viewed as commentaries on the *Spring and Autumn Annals;* the *Rites of Zhou* and the *Book of Etiquette* as supplemental to the *Book of Rites;* and the *Erya* dictionary as an aid to understanding the archaic language of the classics. Others, however, were included in the canon because they were thought to provide important elaborations of truths in the original five. These were the *Analects*, a record of conversations between Confucius (551–479 BCE) and his disciples; the *Mencius*, the writings of Mencius (fourth century BCE) in which he describes his personal audiences with the rulers and ministers of the feudal states and his conversations with his disciples; and the *Classic of Filial Piety*, an account of a dialogue between Confucius and a disciple on the subject of the central virtue of filial piety. But even as the canon filled out to become the Thirteen Classics, the Five Classics remained the central texts. They continued to be the ones to be read first, and the ones to serve as the basis of the civil service examinations until the early years of the fourteenth century.

The Song, a period renowned for its intellectual and cultural vitality generally, proved to be an especially energetic time for classical studies. Literati turned to the classics with an almost missionary commitment. Fervent in the belief that the canon was the repository of truth, the embodiment of all that the great Chinese culture valued, the foremost intellectuals of the early centuries of the Song all dedicated much of their lives to studying the classics and writing commentary on them.[1]

The passion and zeal with which these men and others approached the canon can be accounted for, at least in some part, by the political and intellectual circumstances of the time. To them, the Chinese order, the Chinese way of life, was under threat. The Tang (618–907) empire had collapsed only recently, leaving a once unified realm in a state of fragmentation. The Song, to be sure, had begun the task of rebuilding, but since the founding of the dynasty the Chinese state had been repeatedly invaded and occupied by "barbarian" neighbors to the north and northwest. Just south of the Great Wall, the Song had ceded to the Khitan people and their Liao dynasty (907–1119) sixteen prefectures of Chinese territory in the vicinity of present-day Beijing; in the northwest, the Tangut had established the Xi Xia state (1038–1227), controlling much of Gansu province and the Ordos region south of the Yellow River. (See map on p. xx.) The weakness of the Chinese political and social order thus appeared very real to statesmen and thinkers of the day, who came to trust that a return to right principles, institutions,

---

[1] Fan Zhongyan (989–1052), Hu Yuan (993–1059), Ouyang Xiu (1007–1072), Sima Guang (1019–1086), Zhang Zai (1020–1077), Wang Anshi (1021–1086), Cheng Hao (1032–1085), Cheng Yi (1033–1107), and Su Dongpo (1036–1101), to name but a few.

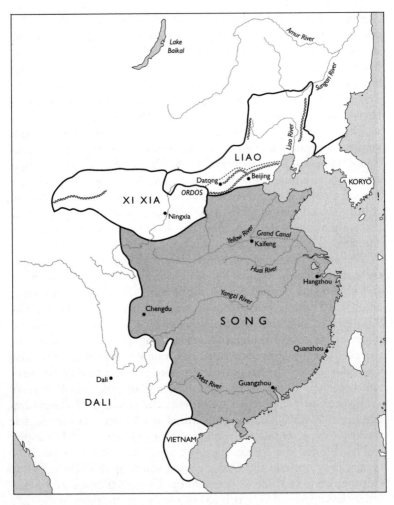

China, *ca.* 1050

techniques of governing, and rites—transmitted in all the writings of the sages—would bring renewed strength to the empire and revitalize the Chinese way of life.

A "barbarian" presence was felt in the intellectual realm as well. Buddhism, which had gained widespread popularity in the Tang, continued to exert influence among all levels of Chinese society. Song literati, echoing the earlier anxiety of the great prose stylist Han Yu 韓愈 (768–824), expressed concerns that Buddhist teachings were tearing asunder the social and moral fabric of the Chinese people. They were especially disturbed by what appeared to be the growing appeal of Chan Buddhism among the intelligentsia, the very people expected to be the defenders of the traditional Confucian order and the leaders of the Chinese state. The persistent and urgent calls by Song literati for the Chinese people to reject the foreign teachings of Buddhism and embrace anew the cherished values of the native tradition did much to fuel the contemporary interest in classical studies.

In the early years of the Song, literati studied and commented extensively on the entire canon of thirteen, giving particular attention to the original five. By the mid-Song, however, their focus began to narrow. They singled out certain texts from among the thirteen: the *Analects* and the *Mencius*, two of the Thirteen Classics, and the *Great Learning* and *Maintaining Perfect Balance*, two brief chapters from the classic *Book of Rites* became, for the literati, an intellectual preoccupation. These were the texts in the canon they found to be especially significant and meaningful, the texts that resonated most strongly with their concerns. By the end of the Song period, these four texts had come to constitute a collection, the Four Books, and had displaced the Five Classics as the authoritative, central texts within the canon. In the early fourteenth century, they would be officially recognized as the basic texts in the civil service examinations, a status they would maintain until the abolition of the examination system in the twentieth century.

This shift from the Five Classics to the Four Books speaks to an essential point: the canon of Thirteen Classics is full of variety. Much as the Bible, with its assortment of books—both in the Old and New Testament—offers a range of teachings with varying

emphases that invite readers to take away a variety of meanings, so
too does the Chinese canon include multiple writings with different
contents and emphases. The Five Classics and the Four Books may
share a fundamental moral, social, and political vision, but the
expression of that vision takes rather different forms in the two
collections. To generalize, the Five Classics illustrate Confucian
morality using concrete examples and lessons from history; set out
ideal institutions and methods of governance drawn from the past;
describe in detail how one should conduct oneself in life's various,
objective situations; and prescribe at length the ritualistic practices
for maintaining a well-ordered society. From these texts the ruler
learns how to rule, the minister learns how to administer the realm,
father and mother learn how to parent, children learn how to express
filial devotion, older and younger learn how to show mutual respect,
and friends learn how to be friends. The Four Books tend to be less
historical, descriptive, and concrete; concerned principally with the
nature of man, the springs or inner source of his morality, and his
relation to the larger cosmos, they are considerably more discursive
and abstract than the Five Classics.

This move away from the Five Classics to the Four Books thus
represents an "inward" shift on the part of literati toward texts in
the canon that treat more deliberately the inner realm of human
morality. This textual shift can no doubt be tied in part to a growing
perception among statesmen and thinkers alike that despite the
most earnest attempts during the eleventh century by activist statesmen such as Fan Zhongyan 范仲淹 and Wang Anshi 王安石 to
introduce specific political and social reforms, to advance practical
measures intended to address the most pressing political, military,
and economic problems facing the dynasty, the empire was nonetheless still in danger. In the late eleventh century and the early twelfth
century, the barbarian menace to the north continued to loom large,
now in the form of the Jurchen tribespeople. The country's economy
remained weak and overburdened, and the Chinese bureaucracy was
embroiled in a bitter, paralyzing factionalism. Looking at the failed
practical attempts at social and political reform, thinkers concluded
that too little attention had been paid by men like Fan and Wang
to the inner sphere, to matters of personal morality, and that

political and social action without a strong moral foundation was simply bound for failure. These thinkers believed that progress in political and social affairs depended on prior progress in the inner sphere of moral self-cultivation. Only good men, only those with the right moral inclinations in the first place, it was supposed, could truly bring about political and social reform that would benefit the people. Given this attitude, it is natural that many literati of the day, studying the classical canon, found themselves attracted to those texts in it that focus on the inner sphere and give priority to the self-cultivation process. It is also natural that, with this inward shift, study of the classics became more philosophical—and less explicitly "results-oriented."

I do not wish to suggest that Confucian literati of the late eleventh century were pushed into this inward shift by political and social realities—or at least the perception of those realities—alone. They were intellectually receptive to the shift in the first place. The writings of Buddhists, especially of the Chan school, had long been addressing such philosophical concerns as human nature, the mind, self-realization, and man's relation to the cosmos—concerns typically associated with the branch of philosophy known as metaphysics. And whereas Confucians had been challenging Buddhists, often fiercely, on particular positions since the Tang dynasty, they nonetheless found the general philosophical concerns raised by Buddhists profoundly appealing and meaningful. By the Song, fruitful and congenial dialogue between Buddhists and Confucians had become commonplace. Indeed, a number of the greatest Confucian literati of the Song not only counted Buddhists among their close acquaintances but themselves had studied Buddhist teachings.[2] In short, many Song Confucians were philosophically predisposed to confront questions about human nature, the source of human morality, self-realization, and the place of man in the cosmos. They were poised for the shift inward.

Like earlier Song literati, Zhu Xi was attracted to the *Analects*, the *Mencius*, the *Great Learning*, and *Maintaining Perfect Balance*. So

---

[2] For instance, Ouyang Xiu, Wang Anshi, Su Dongpo, Zhou Dunyi (1017–1073), Zhang Zai, Cheng Yi, Cheng Hao, and Zhu Xi.

full of meaning were they for him that from 1163 until his death in 1200 he devoted his intellectual energy to preparing, reworking, and refining interlinear commentaries for each of them. During Zhu's lifetime, work on these texts never ceased. Indeed, his traditional biography tells us that three days before his death on April 23, 1200, he was still revising his commentary on the *Great Learning*, a draft of which he had completed as early as 1174. Despite the interest these four texts had generated among literati in the first two centuries of the Song period, Zhu was the first to conceive of them as a coherent collection and publish them together in 1190 as the Four Masters. He was also the first to make the explicit call that they be read before all other classics in the canon, including the long-authoritative Five Classics,[3] thereby heralding a transition from the age of the Five Classics to the age of the Four Books, as the Four Masters would come commonly to be known.

In the Four Books, Zhu Xi believed he had found a subset of classical texts that could constitute an effective "core" curriculum in the Confucian tradition. These Four Books were characterized by, in his words, an "ease, immediacy, and brevity" that ensured that the essential teachings and truths of the Confucian tradition would reach the widest audience possible.[4] To restore the Way (*dao* 道)—socially, politically, and intellectually—the Way had to be made accessible. In his opinion, the full corpus of Thirteen Classics was simply too unwieldy, and the original Five Classics were too lengthy, linguistically archaic and challenging, and, in places, almost incomprehensible. Over and over again in writings and in conversations with disciples and friends, Zhu Xi exhorts students to begin their study of the Way with the Four Books, turning to the Five Classics only once the four had been thoroughly mastered.

Not only did these core texts have an "ease, immediacy, and brevity" that recommended them, but they were also possessed of an authorial pedigree that could not but inspire genuine awe and

---

3 *Zhuzi yulei* (The Conversations of Master Zhu, Arranged Topically) 14.249, i.e., Chapter 14, p. 249. Hereafter the work will be referred to as YL.
4 *Hui'an xiansheng Zhu Wengong wenji* (Collected Literary Works of Master Zhu) 82.26a.

respect. Arguing that the *Great Learning* was a work in two parts, a classic portion by Confucius and a commentary portion by one of his favorite disciples, Zengzi 曾子, and that *Maintaining Perfect Balance* was the work of Zisi 子思, Confucius' grandson, Zhu Xi created for the Four Books an unbroken line of transmission from the great Sage himself to Zengzi, from Zengzi to Zisi, and finally from Zisi to Mencius (hence Zhu's title for the collection, the Four Masters). Whereas Zhu's attribution of authorship, especially in the case of *Maintaining Perfect Balance*, certainly has not gone unquestioned, the Chinese tradition has generally accepted it since the Song dynasty. Thus, in Zhu's hands, the collection came to represent the distilled embodiment of the Sage's teachings and to promise direct access to the minds of the greatest sages of China's past.

In presenting the Four Books in this order—the *Great Learning*, the *Analects*, the *Mencius*, and *Maintaining Perfect Balance*—I am keeping to the particular order prescribed by Zhu Xi and adhered to by the Chinese tradition itself until the twentieth century. Just as Zhu insisted that the Four Books be read first, before the Five Classics and other canonical texts, he insisted, too, that there was a right sequence for reading the Four Books themselves:

> I want men first to read the *Great Learning* to fix upon the pattern of the Confucian Way; next the *Analects* to establish its foundations; next the *Mencius* to observe its development; and next *Maintaining Perfect Balance* to discover the mysteries of the ancients. The *Great Learning* provides within its covers a series of steps and a precise order in which they should be followed; it is easy to understand and so should be read first. Although the *Analects* is concrete, its sayings are scattered about in fragments; on first reading, it is difficult. *Mencius* contains passages that inspire and arouse men's minds. *Maintaining Perfect Balance*, too, is difficult to understand; it should be read only after the other three books.[5]

---

5 YL 14.249

One important pedagogic principle governing this sequence is already familiar to us, for it is one that governed Zhu's decision to privilege the Four Books over the Five Classics: the more accessible text should be read before the less accessible one.

Zhu's pedagogic concerns went beyond telling students what to read and in what order; he was just as anxious that they cultivate the right way to read. To get at the true intentions of the sages, students had to do more than simply pass their eyes over the canonical texts. They had to read each text over and over until they were able to recite it front to back from memory. To read a text fifty or even a hundred times thus was not too many, according to Zhu.[6] He cautioned, however, that the repeated readings must never be allowed to become rote; only if the readings were slow and deliberative, penetrating ever deeper layers of significance, could students "savor" the true flavor of the text and come to appreciate its true taste. In conversation Zhu once described good reading as follows: "You must constantly take the words of the sages and worthies and pass them before your eyes, roll them around and around in your mouth, and turn them over and over in your mind."[7] His hope then was that students would "experience the text personally,"[8] as he was fond of saying, embodying its words and making the sages' teachings their own. He remarked on one occasion: "In reading we must first become intimately familiar with the text so that its words seem to come from our own mouths. We should then continue to reflect on it so that its ideas seem to come from our own minds. Only then can there be real understanding."[9]

The canonical texts, of course, could be difficult to understand, written as they were in an antiquated Chinese, with frequent references to shadowy or unfamiliar people, events, and institutions from China's past. As early as the Han dynasty, scholars perceived the need to provide assistance to students of the classics and began the practice of writing interlinear commentary on them. In this

---

6 YL 10.168.
7 YL 10.162.
8 E.g., YL 10.165, 11.181.
9 YL 10.168.

sort of commentary, they would "interrupt" the classical text, placing elucidating remarks at the end of lines, paragraphs, and passages—wherever they thought it useful or appropriate. The remark might be a simple phonetic or philological gloss on a particular character or two, or it might be a lengthier explanation of the meaning of an entire line or of the philosophical significance of a paragraph or even a chapter. In any event, from the second century BCE on, it became standard practice to read a canonical text with the aid of an accompanying interlinear commentary (see Fig. 6).

Accordingly, the reader here will find that I have interrupted the translation of the Four Books interlinearly, placing commentary at the end of many, if not most, passages. This commentary is largely a summary and explanation of Zhu Xi's understanding of the passages offered in his commentary; it was his understanding, after all, that was declared the standard one by the state in the fourteenth century and as a consequence was required reading for every student of the Four Books. My commentary weaves together a few different types of remarks, all intended to convey to the reader how Zhu—and thus the later Chinese tradition—would have understood these texts. Included are direct citation from and close paraphrase of Zhu's commentary; summary of philosophical points and interpretive exegesis presented by Zhu in his commentary; synthesis of philosophical assumptions and beliefs that implicitly informed Zhu's reading of a passage and are helpful, if not necessary, context for our appreciating his reading of that passage; and my own comments, the purpose of which is to offer interpretive insight into the Four Books, Zhu's standard reading of them, and the *Daoxue* tradition.

The inclusion of commentary in this translation replicates, even if only dimly, the reading experience of the typical Chinese reader. His reading of a canonical text would be constantly interrupted—and informed—by interlinear commentarial remarks. That is, he would read a line of classical text, move to commentary, and, having processed that commentary, proceed to the next line of classical text. This, of course, suggests that the particular commentarial "voice" would shape, rather significantly, the reader's reading and understanding of the classic. By including a commentary that summarizes and explains Zhu's commentary, I hope to show how the genre of

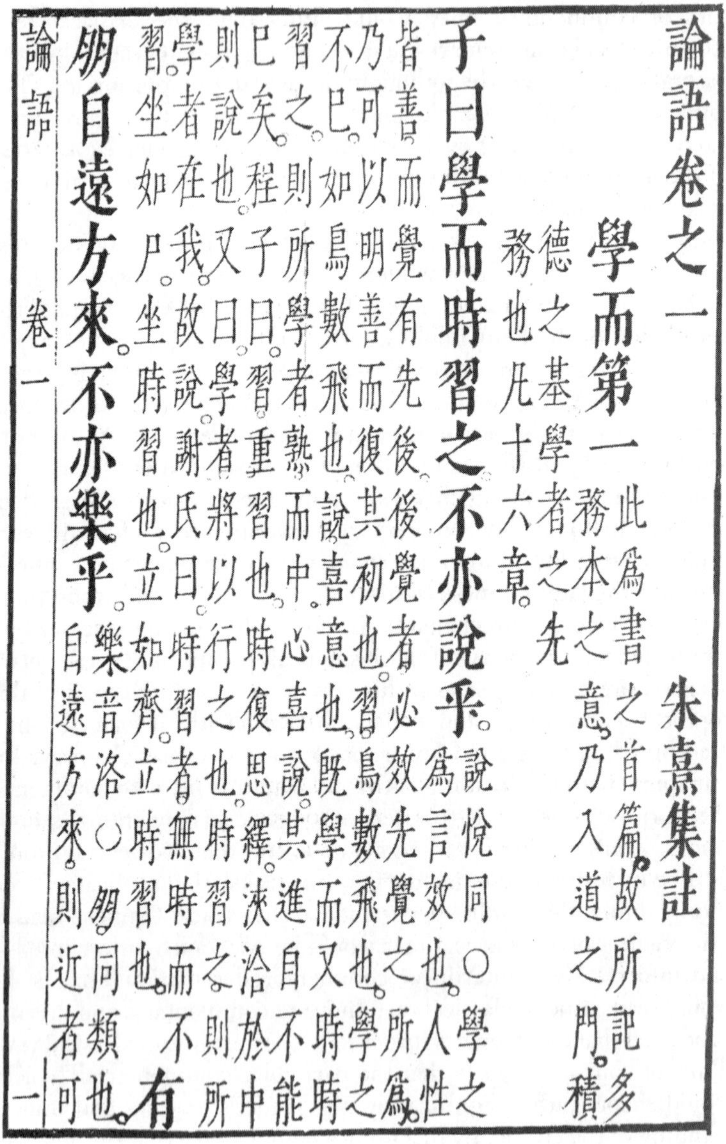

論語卷之一　朱熹集註

學而第一
此爲書之首篇，故所記多務本之意，乃入道之門，積德之基，學者之先也。凡十六章。

子曰：學而時習之，不亦說乎？
說悅同。○學之爲言效也。人性皆善，而覺有先後，後覺者必效先覺之所爲，乃可以明善而復其初也。習，鳥數飛也。學之不已，如鳥數飛也。說，喜意也。既學而又時時習之，則所學者熟，而中心喜說，其進自不能已矣。程子曰：習，重習也。時復思繹，浹洽於中，則說也。又曰：學者將以行之也，時習之，則所學者在我，故說。謝氏曰：時習者，無時而不習。坐如尸，坐時習也；立如齊，立時習也。

朋自遠方來，不亦樂乎？
樂音洛。○朋同類也。自遠方來，則近者可知。有

Fig. 6 Opening page of the *Analects* with Zhu Xi's Commentary. From Zhu Xi, Sishu jangju jizhu.

commentary in general operated in the Chinese classical tradition and, more importantly, how Zhu's commentary on the Four Books in particular shaped the post-1300 literati reading of the Confucian tradition.[10]

Zhu's commentary clearly went a long way in shaping the later imperial Confucian intellectual tradition. Indeed, it shaped the education of every boy aspiring to literacy, of every young Chinese student who ever dreamed of sitting for the civil service examinations. Its influence is hard to overstate. But there is another important reason for including Zhu's commentary in this study of the Four Books: it is in commentary on the Thirteen Classics—especially, of course, on the Four Books—that Zhu is given to the most serious philosophical reflection. It is here that he engages in a sort of dialogue with the great sages of the past. Reading Zhu's commentary enables us to witness his lifelong "conversation" with the venerable teachings of the past and to observe him in the process of meditating on their relevance for him and his contemporaries. Indeed, his commentarial efforts exemplify nicely the sort of fully engaged reading of the writings of the sages that he expects generally of students of the canon. In any event, from this dialogic endeavor comes the unfolding of Zhu's philosophical system known as the "learning of the Way" (*Daoxue*). Often referred to as Neo-Confucianism, it would come to dominate the intellectual landscape of China until the twentieth century.

Thus, through the Four Books and commentary on them by Zhu Xi, readers of this book will be introduced to the central texts in the Chinese tradition for the six-hundred-year period from the fourteenth century to the twentieth century. They will also be exposed to the orthodox reading of these texts during this period, as well as to the dominant values and beliefs of the culture, as embodied in these sacred texts; the standard curriculum in schools and the civil service examinations through the early decades of the

---

[10] For an extended discussion of the role that commentary plays in the Chinese intellectual tradition, and especially its role in shaping the reader's reading of a canonical text, see Daniel K. Gardner, "Confucian Commentary and Chinese Intellectual History."

twentieth century; and the philosophical ideas of China's most influential and commanding thinker since the thirteenth century.[11]

In the translation of the Four Books that follows I have selected passages for inclusion based on three criteria: (1) Is the passage famous? (2) Is the passage, in the judgment of the later Chinese intellectual tradition, essential to the significance of the text? (3) Is the passage, in *my* judgment, central to how we are to understand the later Chinese intellectual tradition? These three criteria often clearly overlap, but a passage need meet only one of them to be included here.

I have based my translation of the Four Books on the Sishu Jizhu (Sibu beiyao edition).

---

11 This introduction has touched on issues taken up more fully in some of my earlier work. The interested reader may refer to "Principle and Pedagogy: Chu Hsi and the Four Books," "Transmitting the Way: Chu Hsi and His Program of Learning," "Confucian Commentary and Chinese Intellectual History," *Learning to Be a Sage*, and *Zhu Xi's Reading of the Analects: Canon, Commentary, and the Classical Tradition*.

THE GREAT LEARNING

THE *GREAT LEARNING*[1] 大學

1. THE WAY OF GREAT LEARNING lies in letting one's inborn luminous virtue shine forth, in renewing the people, and in coming to rest in perfect goodness.

[Zhu Xi's commentary explains that heaven endows all human beings at birth with perfect virtue (*mingde* 明德). The goal for each of us is to give expression to that inborn virtue in everyday life. This requires effort, however. For, just as each of us is born with perfect virtue, so each of us is born with a psychophysical endowment constituted of *qi* 氣, which can perhaps be best understood as the matter and energy that informs and constitutes the entire universe.[2] Unlike the luminous virtue, which is one and the same in all human beings, the particular endowment of psychophysical stuff differs with each individual. This endowment can be more or less balanced, more or less refined, more or less clear. The less balanced, the less refined, the less clear it is, the more likely it will cloud over the individual's innate virtue and keep it from shining forth. Further, the less balanced, the less refined, the less clear the endowment, the more likely it will give rise in the individual to creaturely desires that will inhibit the expression of this inherent virtue.

It is essential to note that no person ever loses the endowed virtue nor does the virtue ever lose its original luminosity or perfection. It

---

1 The *Great Learning*, according to Zhu Xi's arrangement of the text, is divided into eleven chapters: the first chapter, the most important, contains the words of Confucius, and the next ten are a commentary on the "classic portion" prepared by Zengzi, Confucius' disciple. Whereas over the centuries other scholars offered other arrangements of the classic, it was Zhu's that remained the standard. All seven paragraphs of the classic portion are presented here; so too is Chapter 5 of the Zengzi commentary portion.

2 The terms "*qi*," "psychophysical stuff," and "stuff" are used interchangeably throughout this book.

simply becomes obscured. The Way of great learning is the process of bringing balance, refinement, and clarity to our psychophysical endowments so that the inborn virtue in each of us will be unobscured, becoming fully manifest toward others. By manifesting it toward others, we, through the traditional Confucian power of moral example, lead others to engage in a similar process of self-renewal. In short, once we have made our inborn luminous virtue shine forth we are obligated to help bring about the same moral perfection in others.

Zhu's practice of reading and understanding the Four Books in light of contemporary philosophical concerns is apparent in this very first passage of the *Great Learning*.]

2.   Knowing where to come to rest, one becomes steadfast; being steadfast, one may find peace of mind; peace of mind may lead to inner serenity; inner serenity makes reflection possible; only with reflection is one able to reach the resting place.

[Once we recognize where it is that perfect goodness lies, namely, in letting our inborn luminous virtue shine forth and in renewing the people, we feel assured, clear about the direction we are to follow. We become focused and less distracted. Calmness and equilibrium come to prevail. Effective reflection is now possible, and such reflection is sure to lead us to the right place.]

3.   Things have their roots and branches; affairs have a beginning and an end. One comes near the Way in knowing what to put first and what to put last.

[Great learning follows a set order. Making perfect virtue shine forth is the foundation; bringing moral renewal to others grows from it. Similarly, knowledge of what constitutes perfect goodness necessarily comes before its achievement.]

4.   Those of antiquity who wished that all people throughout the empire would let their inborn luminous virtue shine forth put governing their states well first; wishing to govern their states well, they first established harmony in their households; wishing to

establish harmony in their households, they first cultivated themselves; wishing to cultivate themselves, they first set their minds in the right; wishing to set their minds in the right, they first made their intentions true; wishing to make their intentions true, they first extended knowledge to the utmost; the extension of knowledge lies in the investigation of things.

[To bring about moral self-realization in others depends on a program of neatly articulated steps. Cultivation of our own selves makes possible the renewal of others, and self-cultivation itself rests on efforts to investigate things (*gewu* 格物). Thus, the grand Confucian moral agenda—cultivation of the self and the betterment of others—depends on this first step, the investigation of things. But what this classic, the *Great Learning*, means by the term "investigation of things" had long been a matter of debate. Only with the two prominent Neo-Confucian commentators of the twelfth century, Cheng Yi and Zhu Xi, was general agreement reached. Investigation of things for them, and most of the later Chinese tradition, was the process of probing and apprehending the principle (*li* 理) that inheres in each and every thing and affair in the universe. By studying or investigating the principle in all things, we come to understand better the true, underlying nature of those things; and, as our efforts accumulate, our ability to comprehend the world and to relate appropriately—that is, morally—to all things in it deepens.]

5.   Only after things are investigated does knowledge become complete; knowledge being complete, intentions become true; intentions being true, the mind becomes set in the right; the mind being so set, the person becomes cultivated; the person being cultivated, harmony is established in the household; household harmony established, the state becomes well governed; the state being well governed, the empire becomes tranquil.

[Zhu Xi comments that the steps from the investigation of things to cultivation of the self relate to "letting one's inborn luminous virtue shine forth." The steps from establishing harmony in the household to bring tranquility to the empire relate to "renewing the people." He also comments that Confucius was speaking very freely here and that one step in the sorites does not necessarily or automatically lead to the next. In particular, he suggests, advancing from the completion of knowledge to making the intentions true, and from making the intentions true to setting the mind in the right, requires considerable discipline and effort.

This passage, together with the previous one, held special significance for Neo-Confucians. The stress placed on the inner quest for self-perfection and on the role of the mind in that quest resonated strongly with the philosophical concerns that had come to preoccupy literati ever since the middle of the Tang period. At the same time the text remains true to the traditional Confucian responsibility of ordering family, society, and empire. Thus, prominent literati such as Han Yu (768–824) and Li Ao (d. 844) found in the text of the *Great Learning* canonical license to reflect on the process of self-cultivation—without opening themselves to charges that concern with the self was a preoccupation that came at the expense of social commitment.]

6.   From the Son of Heaven on down to commoners, all without exception should regard self-cultivation as the root.

[There are two assertions here. First, self-cultivation (*xiushen* 修身) is to be in no way limited to the elite. Each and every person, irrespective of social, political, and economic status, is to make the effort to refine himself[3] morally, to permit his luminous virtue to shine forth. After all, it is not the Son of Heaven (the traditional Chinese term for the emperor) alone who is endowed with an "inborn luminous virtue." Second, successfully fulfilling the Confucian ideal has its beginnings in the self, in bringing it about that the humanness with which we are all born is unobstructed, luminously manifest to the world.

Late imperial thinkers associated with Neo-Confucianism, men such as Cheng Yi, Zhu Xi, and Wang Yangming (1472–1529), were profoundly committed to the text of the *Great Learning* in large part

---

3 Masculine pronouns have been used consistently throughout all of the texts in this book—within both the translated material and the commentary—in view of the original authors' having written at a time when the readership was almost exclusively male.

because it argues for the applicability of the Confucian self-cultivation process to all people. Any person could practice the program for self-cultivation outlined here; anyone had the potential to manifest perfect humanness and become a sage.]

7. It is impossible that the root be unhealthy and the branches healthy. Never should the important be treated as trivial; never should the trivial be treated as important.

[The root and branch analogy is a common one in the Chinese tradition and is generally used to distinguish between what is the foundation or the basis and what grows out of and depends on the foundation or the basis.

With this passage, what has traditionally been treated as the heart of the *Great Learning,* the portion attributed to Confucius himself, comes to a close. Reading passages #6–7 as a summing up of passages #4–5, Zhu Xi comments: "the 'root' refers to the 'person' and the 'important' refers to the 'family.'" Zhu, with this commentary, is attempting to point up the strong coherence of the text, the close interrelationship among passages within it.

The following passage is part of what Zhu and the later tradition take to be the portion of the *Great Learning* in which Confucius' disciple Zengzi offers his commentary on the words of his Master. In studying and reflecting on this portion, Zhu Xi concluded that its original fifth chapter, the Zengzi commentary on "the investigation of things" and "the completion of knowledge," had been lost and so he "reconstructed" it. Ever since, the Chinese tradition has regarded this, the "supplemental" fifth chapter by Zhu Xi, as part of the body of the *Great Learning,* and indeed as the most important chapter in the text next to the portion above by Confucius himself:]

What is meant by "the extension of knowledge lies in the investigation of things" is this: If we wish to extend our knowledge to the utmost, we must probe thoroughly the principle in those things that we encounter. Now every person's intellect is possessed of the capacity for knowing; at the same time every thing in the world is possessed of principle. To the extent that principle is not thoroughly probed a person's knowledge is not fully realized. For this reason, the first step of instruction in the *Great Learning* teaches students that, encountering anything at all in the world, they must build on what they already know of principle and probe still deeper, until they reach its limit. Exerting themselves in this manner for a long time, they will one day suddenly become all penetrating; this being the case, the manifest and the hidden, the subtle and the obvious qualities of all things will all be known, and the mind, in its whole substance and vast operations, will be completely illuminated. This is what is meant by "the investigation of things." This is what is meant by "the completion of knowledge."

[Zhu Xi, in "filling in the lacuna" here, as he puts it, lays out the metaphysical foundations of his Neo-Confucian vision of self-cultivation. It is a process of self-cultivation available to everyone, as everyone has the faculty for knowing. The process requires that this faculty for knowing, in all affairs, relationships, and things in the universe, seeks to understand principle; over time such investigation of principle in the affairs, relationships, and things around us can result in a full understanding of the universe, of what gives coherence and real meaning to the universe and everything in it. It should be pointed out that the ultimate goal of the Neo-Confucian program of self-cultivation is not the understanding of the true nature of things. The goal is moral action, moral behavior: on the basis of having probed and understood principle, we know precisely how to comport ourselves as required by the nature of everything that we encounter. In all of life's situations we behave as we should interrelationally. Thus, as outlined in #4–5 in the portion by Confucius, we can readily bring good governance and harmony to family, state, and empire.

If in fact there was a lost fifth chapter, it is safe to observe that it would not have been expressed in the terms Zhu Xi uses here. Principle and the search for it only became part of the Confucian vocabulary with thinkers associated with the "learning of the Way," or the Neo-Confucian movement, in the eleventh and twelfth centuries. Nonetheless, from the time of Zhu on, this passage would be read as a chapter of the classic itself, replacing the "lost chapter" transmitted by Zengzi and his disciples.]

THE ANALECTS

THE ANALECTS[4] 論語

1. The Master said, To learn and rehearse it constantly, is this indeed not a pleasure? To have friends come from afar, is this indeed not a delight? Others do not know him, yet he feels no resentment, is he indeed not a superior man? (1.1)

[This is the opening passage of the text of the *Analects*. We are alerted right off to the emphasis that will be placed on learning throughout the classic. And whereas Confucius himself does not make very specific the sort of learning he has in mind, Zhu Xi does. It is worth citing his commentary briefly: "To learn means 'to emulate.' Human nature (*xing* 性) is good in everyone, but some are awakened to it before others. Those awakened to it later must emulate what those awakened earlier do. Only then can they understand goodness and return to their original state." Learning is thus learning to be moral. And whereas learning, for Zhu, most certainly includes the study of canonical texts, it also refers to learning through a deliberate emulation of morally exemplary persons.

Zhu introduces a philosophical premise here that would have been unfamiliar to earlier readers: human nature is in all cases good, and through effort, through learning, it can be given full expression in everyday life. Zhu lays out the premise here, and it opens the door to understanding his readings of all that follows in the *Analects*. Already it should be clear that Zhu eagerly seeks to find coherence between and among the Four Books. That human nature is good in each and every person is the meaning Zhu finds in the *Great Learning*, notably in passage #1. And that this nature must be cultivated through learning is

4 The *Analects* is made up of twenty rather brief "books," which are divided into "chapters." The notation in parenthesis at the end of each passage here refers to the traditional book and chapter number, as found in the *Lunyu yinde*, published in the Harvard-Yenching Institute Sinological Index Series.

11

the entire point of "the investigation of things" found in #4–5 of the same text.

That friends come from afar is testimony to the powerful attraction that a perfectly moral person has on others. The commentary remarks, "Extend goodness to others, and those who trust and follow will be many."

The superior man (*junzi* 君子) cares not whether others know and acknowledge him. For him, "Learning rests with oneself; being known or not rests with others. How can there be resentment?"

The reading proposed by Zhu here would become, by the thirteenth century, the standard interpretation and the required understanding of the text among candidates for the civil service examinations.]

2.   Youzi [a disciple] said, One who is of filial and fraternal character but at the same time loves defying superiors is rare indeed. One who does not love defying superiors but at the same time loves sowing disorder has never existed. The superior man attends to the root. The root having been established, the Way issues forth. And filial piety and fraternal respect—are they not the root of practicing true goodness? (1.2)

[True goodness is foundational to our human nature. The issue here for Neo-Confucians is how to give expression to this goodness. Taking the line that true goodness is the substance of our human nature and filial piety and fraternal respect its function, they reason that to be filial and to have fraternal respect in the family is to put into practice the goodness that is our human nature.[5] In turn, the filial and fraternal respect in the family gets expressed in our extra-familial relations as "true goodness and love." This is why the Master says: "The root having been established, the Way issues forth. And filial piety and fraternal respect—are they not the root of practicing true goodness?"]

3.   The Master said, Clever words and ingratiating looks—seldom are they associated with true goodness. (1.3)

---

5 It was traditional for Chinese philosophers to speak of a thing's substance (*ti* 體) and function (*yong* 用); it was for them a distinction between the constituent of a thing and the practice of the thing or the use to which the thing is put.

[Such speech and appearance are intended to please others; they are not genuine expressions of one's innate virtue.]

4.   Zengzi said, Every day I examine my own person on three counts: In working on behalf of others, have I failed to be true to myself? In my associations with friends, have I failed to be true to my word? As for what has been passed on to me, have I failed to rehearse it? (1.4)

[Zengzi, a prominent disciple of the Master, was deeply admired by later Confucians, in particular for the emphasis he placed on the "inner life" of the individual. Constant self-examination is the source of moral perfection, for him. Note that being true to the principles of one's good nature, practicing them in the form of true goodness, righteousness, propriety, and wisdom, is the foundation.]

5.   Worry not that others do not know you; worry lest you do not know others. (1.16)

[A good man looks within himself and thus does not need the recognition of others; he must, however, be capable of discerning between right and wrong, and falsehood and truth—this is what is meant by to "know others."]

6.   The Master said, One who practices government by virtue may be compared to the North Star: it remains in its place while the multitude of other stars turn toward it. (2.1)

[Virtue (*de* 德) in the ruler exercises a moral power over those he governs; this virtue operates silently and without force, through a sort of charismatic attraction. Virtue's capacity to exert influence over others, even to transform them, is spoken of repeatedly throughout the *Analects*. The truly good person and the superior man are said by Confucius to have the wherewithal to move others morally. In this passage it is the ideal ruler who is the subject.]

7.   The Master said, Lead them with tools of government, regulate them by punishment, and the people will avoid punishment but have

no sense of shame. Lead them with virtue, regulate them by ritual, and they will have a sense of shame and moreover arrive at good. (2.3)

[Again, Confucius speaks to the moral power of the ruler. He is resisting a contemporary, sixth-century BCE trend away from government based on family-like relations toward government impersonal and less familial in nature, one based on codes of laws and punishments. Why is rule by virtue effective? According to Zhu Xi and other Neo-Confucians, since virtue is embodied in human nature, and since all of us are born with precisely the same human nature, the ruler's expression of virtue stimulates the virtue inborn in each of us. This is to say then that rule by virtue does not simply create order among the people; it has the power to awaken in us our innate nature so that we may "arrive at good." This passage then speaks powerfully to the belief that ideal Confucian rule goes beyond the ordering of the sociopolitical realm; Confucian rule brings about moral transformation in the people. Now, why is ritual (*li* 禮) necessary as well? The Neo-Confucian answer is cast in the terms of the day: Virtue is an effective means of transforming many people, but those people whose allotment of psychophysical stuff is of a lower quality need the more concrete example of ritual.

As this analect underscores, ritual is a central feature of the Confucian vision, valued as the outward expression of true goodness. But its precise role in that vision varies with different Confucian thinkers. For some, most notably perhaps the early philosopher Xunzi, this outward expression works to shape the individual into a fully humane being; for others, such as Zhu Xi, ritual practice is more the natural social expression of a being who by nature is already fully humane.

This analect deserves special attention as it expresses an ideal deeply held by Confucius: Good government is that which resorts least to laws and punishments.]

8.   The Master said, At fifteen, I set my mind-and-heart[6] on learning. At thirty, I stood on my own. At forty, I had no doubts. At fifty,

---

6 "Mind-and-heart" is the translation for *xin* 心; in the Chinese tradition the character refers both to the source of intellect and understanding and the center of emotions and feelings.

I knew heaven's decree. At sixty, my ears were in accord. At seventy, I followed the desires of my mind-and-heart without overstepping right. (2.4)

[Confucius presents here his moral autobiography. But clearly it is meant to be more than autobiography. It is a sequential template for learning for all students of the Way. Setting the mind-and-heart on learning is the foundation. That is, the student must have the will, the determination, to embark on the Confucian path. Confucius never explains how to cultivate this will, nor does he explain why some people develop it and others do not. But, without it, a person will not arrive at moral perfection.

Moral perfection, the outcome of the learning process begun by Confucius at fifteen years of age, is founded, according to the Zhu commentary on this passage, on coming to know heaven's decree. And, interestingly, the commentary's gloss of "to know heaven's decree" is "to probe principle (*qiongli* 窮理) and fully realize human nature." Thus, whatever the Master's intention here, Neo-Confucians link the realization of sagehood to the process of probing principle, and consequently the text of the *Analects* to the text of the *Great Learning* (#4–5). Finally, probing principle is associated by Neo-Confucians with the realization of the innately good nature, which in turn guarantees total understanding of the true and perfect practice of it.]

9.   Ziyou [a lesser-known disciple] asked about filial piety. The Master said, Nowadays to be "filial" means simply to be capable of providing parents with nourishment. But even dogs and horses get their nourishment from us. Without the feeling of reverence, what difference is there? (2.7)

[This point is repeated throughout the *Analects:* There must be genuine feeling behind the form. All rites, all interactions with others, must be performed with a feeling of respect, a feeling of reverence, to be authentic. The outer must be a faithful expression of the inner. Filiality (*xiao* 孝) is the topic here, but throughout the text Confucius extends this principle to performance of the spectrum of rites.]

10.   The Master said, The superior man is not a utensil. (2.12)

[The superior man has no one skill or use but is superior by virtue of exercising morality and true goodness in all situations.]

11.   Zigong [a well-known disciple] asked about the superior man. The Master said, Practice comes before the preaching; only then does the preaching follow. (2.13)

[Confucius' response, according to Zhu, is based on his assessment of Zigong's character. That is, Zigong finds preaching easy but practicing hard.]

12.   The Master said, You [also called Zilu, a disciple known more as a man of action than a man of learning], shall I teach you about knowing? To know it and to recognize that you know it; not to know it and to recognize that you do not know it. This is knowing. (2.17)

[This is an exhortation aimed at the questioner, Zilu, in particular. Confucius thought Zilu was always a bit too bold and certain, even about those things he did not know. But it serves as admonition to all of us more generally.]

13.   Duke Ai asked, What can be done so that the people will be obedient? The Master responded, Raise up the straight, place them over the crooked, and the people will be obedient; raise up the crooked, place them over the straight, and the people will not be obedient. (2.19)

[The virtue of the ruler entails recognizing and choosing the right men to serve him. Indeed, what enables him to remain inactive (cf. #90) and stay in his place (cf. #6) is that upright officials do the administrative work of governing on his behalf.]

14.   The Master said, If he is a man (ren 人) but not truly good (ren 仁), what does he have to do with ritual? If he is a man but not truly good, what does he have to do with music? (3.3)

[Confucius speaks frequently of music in the *Analects*. For him, music had the function of ritual, which both promotes harmony in man and serves to express the inner harmony he embodies.

Zhu's commentary reads this passage to mean that ritual and music can be harmonious and efficacious only when performed by the person who has successfully retained his original mind-and-heart. That is, proper performance of ritual and music is the outer expression of the cultivated goodness within.]

15. Liu Fang asked about the fundamentals of ritual. The Master said, A big question indeed. In ritual, it is better to be frugal than extravagant; in mourning rites, it is better to be sorrowful than meticulous. (3.4)

[More important than display of ritual are the feelings behind it. Here, according to Zhu Xi, the feelings of reverence and of grief take precedence over ritual ornamentation.]

16. The Master said, The neighborhood True Goodness is most beautiful. If by choice one does not come to settle in True Goodness—how can one become wise? (4.1)

[According to Zhu Xi, the point is not so much that such a person is unwise for having chosen the inappropriate neighborhood. Rather, it is that this person, having settled in a place where the truly good do not dwell, is at risk of "losing the original mind-and-heart that distinguishes between right and wrong." This passage speaks to the power of moral example: surrounded by good we may more easily learn the good; surrounded by the not good we may more easily lose touch with our original nature.]

17. The Master said, Wealth and official rank are what every man desires. If he comes by them undeservedly, he will not abide in them. Poverty and low station are what every man detests. If he comes by them undeservedly, he does not avoid them. The superior man who departs from true goodness, how does he fulfill the name? The superior man does not depart from true goodness for the space of

a single meal. In times of haste he keeps to it, and in times of confusion he keeps to it. (4.5)

[A person must hold on to true goodness at all times. To achieve wealth or position only by departing from it is, of course, unacceptable; at the same time, if one finds oneself impoverished and in humble straits, in spite of one's adherence to true goodness, so be it.]

18.   The Master said, I for one have never seen a person who loved the truly good or a person who hated what is not truly good. He who loves the truly good puts nothing ahead of it; he who hates what is not truly good practices the truly good and does not let what is not truly good get near his person. Is there anyone capable for the span of a single day of devoting himself to the truly good? I for one have never seen one whose strength is not capable of it. I suppose there are such people, but I for one have never seen one. (4.6)

[Here we return to the point made above—it is not a deficiency of strength that prevents us from practicing true goodness, but rather a deficiency of will or desire. To be empathetic toward another requires little expenditure of energy; indeed, to be empathetic even for an entire day poses no special challenge to a person's strength. The problem is that we do not fix our will, we do not firm up our determination to practice empathy in each and every one of our encounters with others.

Sure, when we first awake we might behave with true familial affection toward a parent or a sibling; later in the morning we might reach out with heartfelt compassion to a friend worried about her ailing dog; in the early afternoon we might with selfless sympathy go to the aid of a starving or infirm stranger; and in the evening we might with all sincerity extend ourselves to a roommate who returns home distressed by a poor academic performance or a failing relationship. But to practice genuine empathy in all of these daily interactions, not to mention the less significant ones with the mail carrier, the boss, and the waitperson, requires sustaining our determination and devotion without the slightest interruption. This is where the difficulty lies.]

19. The Master said, Shen! My Way has one thread running through it. Zengzi said, Yes, of course. The Master left and his disciples asked, What did he mean? Zengzi said, The Way of our Master is being true to oneself and empathetic toward others, nothing more. (4.15)

[The message of this passage echoes that of the last. If the Master's teachings are about any one thing, it is the practice of empathy (*shu* 恕), Zengzi suggests. But, here empathy is accompanied by the character *zhong* 忠, which Neo-Confucians of the Song understood as "giving full expression to oneself." For them, being true to oneself is being true to our innate good nature and realizing that nature through the self-cultivation process. Zhu's commentary cites Master Cheng: "Being true to oneself is to be without falsehood; being empathetic toward others is the means by which to put being true to oneself in actual practice. Being true to oneself is substance; being empathetic toward others is function." This passage recalls the first line of the *Great Learning* (#1), in which the student is called upon to let his inborn luminous virtue shine forth and then give expression to it in his relations with others.

A note about the reference here to "Master Cheng": Zhu Xi was a devoted student of the teachings of both Cheng Hao and Cheng Yi, the two great philosopher brothers of the eleventh century, and even edited a collection of their sayings, *Henan Chengshi yishu*. Whereas Zhu had closer philosophical affinities with the younger of the two, Cheng Yi, and whereas together their teachings would become known as the Cheng-Zhu school of *Daoxue*, or Neo-Confucianism, he admired both brothers deeply. As early as the thirteenth century, Zhao Shunsun (1215–1276) remarked that since Zhu considered the teachings of the brothers to be sufficiently similar, in citing them in his commentary on the Four Books he did not feel it necessary to distinguish between them and instead used the collective "Master Cheng."[7]]

20. The Master said, The superior man understands righteousness; the small person understands profit. (4.16)

---

7 *Lunyu zuanshu*, "LunMeng gangling" 4a.

[The distinction in the *Analects* between the superior man and the small person is not socioeconomic—as it had been earlier in the Chinese tradition. The terms, for Confucius, mark a moral distinction, between the person who has chosen to follow the Way and the person who has not. For another important passage on righteousness and profit, see the *Mencius* 1.]

21.   When you see a worthy man, think about equaling him. When you see an unworthy man, look within yourself. (4.17)

[Whether truly worthy or not, others can be our teachers. With self-reflection, the worthy teach us what to emulate, and the unworthy teach us what is in need of correction in our own selves.]

22.   The Master said, The superior man desires to be slow in word but quick in deed. (4.24)

23.   The Master said, Virtue never dwells alone; it is sure to have neighbors. (4.25)

[Another passage that speaks of the power of moral suasion, its ability to attract others.]

24.   The Master said to Zigong, Of you and Hui [Yan Hui, the Master's most beloved disciple], who is the better? He responded, Me? How could I dare compare myself to Hui? Hui hears one matter and understands ten; I hear one matter and understand two. The Master said, You are not his equal. I grant you, you are not his equal. (5.9)

[Yan Hui is praised here for his intellectual prowess, his ability to extend inferentially the significance of what he has heard. This is one of many passages in which Confucius expresses his profound respect and admiration for Yan Hui. The message of the passage is similar to the one in #38, where Confucius expresses the expectation that students will go beyond the one corner he shows them to understand the other three.

The commentary on the last line is a simple example of how Zhu will gloss a character or line quite differently from earlier commentators.

Most commentators take the *yu* 與 ("grant") in the last line to mean "and," and the whole line to mean, "Neither you nor I is his equal." But Zhu reads this *yu* as *xu* 許, understanding it to mean "allow" or "grant."]

25. Ji Wenzi [a minister of the state Lu] would act only after considering it three times. Upon hearing of this, the Master said, Twice is sufficient. (5.20)

[The commentary cites Master Cheng's remark that by the third time selfish thoughts are likely to enter into the consideration. Zhu adds that whereas the superior man is attentive to probing principle, he values decisiveness as well.]

26. The Master said, Sadly, I have yet to meet a person who can see his own faults and in his own mind bring the charges against himself. (5.27)

[To be a superior man is not to be without faults; rather, it is to confront them and in one's own mind-and-heart accept responsibility for them. Clearly, only then can one correct the faults and morally improve oneself. Zhu Xi understands the *nei* 內 ("inner") here to refer to the mind-and-heart and says that acceptance of responsibility must be genuine, not simply a matter of words.

We are quick to recognize the faults in others, much slower to accept them in ourselves.]

27. The Master said, In a hamlet of ten households, there are sure to be those who in loyalty and trustworthiness are my equal—but none who are my equal in love of learning. (5.28)

[Cultivating loyalty and trustworthiness is relatively easy; far more difficult is hearing the Way and thereby becoming a sage. It is possible, but only through the most dedicated learning. Zhu, understanding the passage as he does, is suggesting that embodying the Way and achieving sagehood are in theory attainable by anyone, but only on the condition that the person engage in the most rigorous program of learning.

"Those who do not engage in learning cannot avoid becoming mere rustics," the commentary concludes.]

28. Duke Ai asked who among the disciples loves learning. The Master responded, There was Yan Hui! He loved learning. Never did he transfer his anger; never did he repeat a mistake. Unfortunately, the time allotted to him was short and he died. Now there is no one. Nor have I yet to hear of one who loves learning. (6.2)

[Yan Hui's self-cultivation was such that his anger was always well placed, arising in response to a particular matter or situation and never transferred to another; also, so sensitive had the learning process made him to right and wrong that he would never commit even the slightest transgression twice. With Hui's death, Confucius opines here, there is none among his disciples who could be said to love learning. Even more, Confucius has heard of no one outside his circle of disciples who has a reputation for a love of learning.]

29. The Master said, Hui! For three months his mind-and-heart would not depart from true goodness. As for others, they might be up to it once a day or once a month, but that is all. (6.7)

[Passage #18 speaks of the difficulty of devoting oneself to true goodness even "for the span of a single day."]

30. The Master said, Worthy indeed was Hui! A bowlful of food; a ladleful of drink; a shabby alleyway. Others would have found it unbearably miserable. But for Hui, it did nothing to alter his pleasure. Worthy indeed was Hui! (6.11)

31. The Master said, Who can go out except by the door? Why is it that no one follows along this Way? (6.17)

[Everyone appreciates that in leaving a house there is but one way out—by the door. But few indeed are those who appreciate that in living life there is but one way to follow—*the* Way.]

32.   The Master said, The wise person delights in water; the truly good person delights in mountains. The wise person is active; the truly good person is inactive. The wise person is joyful; the truly good person enjoys long life. (6.23)

[The wise (*zhizhe* 知者) penetrate the principle of everything and flow everywhere. Being like water, they take delight in it. The truly good (*renzhe* 仁者) take their rest in moral principle, never wavering, never moving. Being like a mountain they take delight in mountains. Active without any constraints, the wise person is joyful. Inactive and constant, the truly good person enjoys long life.

This remark by Confucius is oft cited by the tradition, but commentators are at odds to explain it and find little to agree upon. Zhu Xi, as he so often does, reads the passage in terms of his Song metaphysics. The wise person, who probes principle everywhere, is joyful in pursuit of moral perfection; the truly good person, having achieved moral perfection, naturally acts just as he should in dealing with life, and thus finds life serene and peaceful.]

33.   The superior man who learns widely in the culture and keeps to the essential through ritual surely will not transgress. (6.27)

[Broad familiarity with and understanding of the Chinese cultural tradition is important if one is to learn to sort out good from bad, and right from wrong. But only if one keeps oneself in line with the good and the right, in accord with the principle in things and by means of ritual practice, will broad learning be put in service of the Way.]

34.   Zigong said, Suppose there was one who widely bestowed benefits on the people and was capable of bringing relief to the multitude. What would you say? Could he be called truly good? The Master said, Why just truly good? Wouldn't he surely be a sage? Even Yao and Shun would find this difficult. Now wishing himself to be established, the truly good person establishes others; and, wishing himself to achieve prominence, he makes others prominent. The ability to draw analogies from what is near at hand can be called the way to true goodness. (6.30)

[The disciples are constantly pressing their Master for a definition—or at least a clearer understanding—of true goodness. The Master, as in #19, suggests that true goodness lies somewhere in the direction of the ability to empathize, the ability to gauge others—their feelings and needs—by taking stock of oneself. This is what is meant by "to draw analogies from what is near at hand." What makes this possible, from the Neo-Confucian perspective, is that all human beings are similar in their humanity, having been endowed with the same good nature. See also #94.]

35.   The Master said, I transmit and create nothing of my own. I put my trust in and love the ancients. I would venture to compare myself to our Old Peng. (7.1)

["Old Peng," according to Zhu Xi, refers to the worthy official of the Shang dynasty (c. 1600–c. 1050 BCE) who enjoyed telling stories from the past.

    Confucius is insistent here that he is nothing more than a transmitter, a person only interested in the past and intent on passing it on to later generations. Clearly, then, the past for him is worth passing on; it was a time, in his view, when the Way prevailed in Chinese society. In learning about the institutions, the political and social norms, and the cultural customs of the past, he and others might have hoped to reinvigorate Chinese society and save it from its deplorable state. Found throughout Confucius' remarks is an idealization of the past, a belief that in the early years of the Zhou dynasty (c. 1050–221 BCE) a perfect society prevailed. Confucius' hope was, through devoted study of it, to resuscitate the China of the past and bring about another golden age, a time of perfect harmony and prosperity. This, of course, is why government and rites/customs play such a central role in the *Analects* (see #7). Of course, the question remains whether the early Zhou was indeed such a golden age. The evidence available to us at the moment is insufficient to draw conclusions. But the point is that with Confucius' idealization of the past, the past became the ideal.]

36.   The Master said, How my fortunes have declined! It has been awhile now since I last dreamt that I saw the Duke of Zhou. (7.5)

[The meaning of this passage, following on the previous passage, should be clear. Confucius feels a strong affinity with the Duke of Zhou, who, as the younger brother of King Wu and the regent for King Wu's successor, King Cheng, had been responsible for putting the Way into practice in the early years of the Zhou. When young, Confucius was so determined to implement the Way of the Duke of Zhou that he would dream of meeting the Duke in person. But now that he is older and has concluded that he is incapable of putting it into practice, his hopes have diminished and he no longer dreams of the Duke.]

37. Never have I refused instruction to one who of his own accord comes to me, though it be with as little as a bundle of dried meat. (7.7)

[It was customary for a new student to bring a gift to his teacher. Only the very poorest students would bring bundled strips of dried meat. Zhu explains that because every person is endowed with the same good nature, Confucius would happily teach anyone, even the poorest, in the hope that that person would "enter into goodness."]

38. The Master said, Those not anxious I do not instruct; those not eager I do not enlighten. If I raise up one corner and they do not come back with the other three, I do not continue. (7.8)

[The theme of learning continues. In deciding which students to take on, Confucius looks for an eagerness to learn; only once he is assured that they possess the will and the determination to see the learning through to self-perfection does he teach them. Master Cheng remarks in Zhu's commentary that the eagerness shown on students' faces and in their words reveals their true intentions (spoken of in *Great Learning* #4–5).]

39. The Master said, I am not one who was born knowing it. I am one who loves antiquity and is quick to seek it there. (7.20)

[One born knowing it is one born with the most perfect allotment of psychophysical stuff, so pure and refined that moral principle is self-evident, without any effort or learning. This may be modesty on the Master's part, but the remark is no doubt also intended as an exhortation to others to pursue the path of learning. In commentary, Neo-Confucians insist that Confucius was indeed born knowing it, that is, moral principle; nonetheless, he had to look to the ancients to learn about ritual, music, names and things, and the changing affairs, past and present.]

40. The Master said, Walking in a group of three, I am sure to have teachers. I pick out the good points and follow them and the bad points and change them in myself. (7.22)

[For students eager to learn, eager to improve morally, everyone is a teacher. The behavior of others serves as a mirror. Observing the good and the bad points in others, students become aware of those virtues they must cultivate in themselves (see #1, which calls for students to follow the lead of those who have earlier become aware of their goodness) as well as the flaws in themselves that are in need of correcting. Being with others is an opportunity then for self-scrutiny.

This passage reminds us that learning entails more than book learning. In a sense, Confucius is as much an ethnographer as a student of the classical writings that have come down to him. In observing others, he is determining for himself, and presumably for those he is teaching, the cultural traits and customs most worthy of preserving and transmitting.]

41. The Master taught four things: culture, conduct, doing one's best, and being true to others. (7.25)

[The term *zhong* 忠 is glossed by Neo-Confucians in the various passages in the *Analects* as "doing one's best" or "being true to oneself" (cf. #19). "Being true to oneself" is to be true to our innate, good nature. It is, then, to do our best, to give expression to the good that is within us. Master Cheng comments here that the Master taught people "to study culture (*wen* 文), to refine one's conduct, and to hold on to doing one's best and being true to others. Doing one's best and being true to others are the root."]

42. The Master said, Is true goodness indeed so far away? If I desired true goodness, true goodness would be right at hand. (7.30)

[True goodness (*ren* 仁) is the highest virtue in the Master's teachings, the one that subsumes all others. Yet, nowhere in the *Analects* does the Master offer a precise definition of it. In conversing with disciples he frequently characterizes a particular behavior as *ren* behavior, but he is reluctant to go beyond the situational characterization to a fixed definition of the term. The orthography of the character offers some help. The character consists of two components, one meaning "person" (人) and the other meaning "two" (二), suggesting that one is *ren*, or truly good, only in relation to other human beings. It is a communal virtue: to treat others in a truly good manner. But what does treating others in a truly good manner entail in practice? Two previous passages (#19 and #34) provide guidance. True goodness refers to something like the ability, in all interactions with others, to practice empathy, to put oneself in their shoes; that is, in all of life's situations, to treat others with genuine respect, as one would wish to be treated oneself.

"Is true goodness indeed so far away?" suggests, of course, that for Confucius it is not. The question is, why then do so few people exhibit it? Confucius supplies his own answer: their will or desire is insufficient. But what makes it "right at hand" in the first place? Confucius never says. But Zhu Xi and other Neo-Confucians do: we are, after all, endowed with a good nature at birth, which Mencius, in the next of the Four Books, argues contains the seeds of true goodness, together with righteousness, propriety, and wisdom. Drawing on Mencius, the Neo-Confucians concluded that true goodness was right there, in our innate nature, waiting to shine forth (See also *Great Learning* #1).]

43. The Master said, As for sageliness and true goodness—can I possibly claim these for myself? Still it can be said that I work at them tenaciously and teach them to others tirelessly, nothing more. Gongxi Hua [a disciple said to be especially conversant with ritual] said, This, alas, is just what we disciples are unable to learn. (7.34)

[Gongxi Hua is suggesting that if the Master is tireless in his practice and teaching of sageliness and true goodness but still cannot possibly claim to have achieved them, how can the disciples be capable of learning them?

So difficult is it, in Confucius' view, to become a truly good person that throughout the *Analects* he resists the suggestion that he himself has succeeded in becoming one.]

44.   The Master said, The superior man is calm and at ease; the small person is constantly apprehensive. (7.37)

[The reason for these different states of mind is simple, the commentary, citing Master Cheng, would have us believe. The superior man accords with principle and consequently is always relaxed, whereas the lesser person is a slave to material things and thus often distressed and agitated. Confucius here simply provides another characteristic of the superior man. Zhu, however, goes beyond mere characterization, explaining what it is that enables the superior man to be "calm and at ease." Drawing on Song metaphysics, he suggests that the superior man accords with principle (*li*) in all of his dealings, whereas the lesser man is encumbered by creaturely desires.]

45.   Zengzi said, A gentleman must be broad and resolute, for the burden is heavy and the journey is long. He takes true goodness as his burden: is that not indeed heavy? And only with death does he stop: is that not indeed long? (8.7)

[Only with death does the challenge of achieving true goodness stop. This is a telling point. Achieving true goodness is not the same as achieving a state of total and perpetual enlightenment. Rather, true goodness must, in a sense, be achieved over and over and over again. That is, in each and every encounter in life, a person must will to true goodness, treating others genuinely empathetically, as he would wish to be treated himself. If in any particular encounter, he gives up this will and does not extend himself perfectly appropriately, for that moment at least, he is no longer truly good. The vigilance must be constant and lifelong.]

46.   The Master said, People can be made to follow it, but they cannot be made to understand it. (8.9)

[The Neo-Confucian commentary glosses this passage to mean that people can be made to follow "principle as it should be," that is, the Way. That they "cannot be made to understand it" does not mean that they cannot understand it—for, in fact, all people are capable of understanding. It means instead that it is up to the individual, it is his choice to come to understand it or not. An individual who does not will to understand cannot be made or forced to understand. This reading departs from the earlier traditional reading, which took *min* 民 ("people") to mean "the common people" and the passage to mean that the common people simply are not capable of understanding the Way.]

47. The Master said, To study for three years without fancying an official salary—such a person is not easy to find. (8.12)

[This echoes the earlier point that learning, ideally, is for the sake of oneself, that is, for the purpose of moral improvement, not as a means to office or some other material end.]

48. Be firm in commitment and fond of learning; be content to die and adept at the Way. Do not enter a state in danger; do not reside in a state in disorder. When the Way prevails under heaven, show yourself; when the Way does not prevail, remain hidden. When the Way prevails in the state, be ashamed of being poor and humble; when the Way does not prevail in the state, be ashamed of being wealthy and of high rank. (8.13)

[Only the individual firm in commitment, fond of learning, prepared to die for what is right, and who is a follower of the Way will remain hidden and not show himself when the Way does not prevail. Others are eager to serve under any conditions. But should the Way prevail, the person of principle has no choice but to serve.]

49. The Master said, Study as though you will not catch up to it, as though you fear even losing sight of it. (8.17)

50. The Master rarely spoke of profit, of fate, or of true goodness. (9.1)

[Profit harms righteousness; the principle of fate is much too abstruse; and the Way of true goodness is much too large.]

51.   The Master was entirely free of four things. He was not (*wu* 毋) selfish, insistent, stubborn, or egotistical.[8] (9.4)

[These four are all related, with the latter three all arising from selfishness. Selfishness leads to insistence, which becomes lodged in stubbornness, which in turn becomes total egotism.]

52.   The Master said, Do I possess knowledge? No, I do not. Some vulgar fellow put a question to me and my mind drew a blank, so I thrashed the matter out, from one end to the other, leaving nothing unturned. (9.8)

[This saying picks up on the frequent theme that it is not some sort of superior intelligence or knowledge but rather the determined pursuit of learning that distinguishes the Master, the great Sage, from others. All of us are to cultivate this sort of determination. The passage also speaks to the Master's general willingness to engage anyone interested in learning from him.]

53.   Zigong said, Here I have this precious jade. Do I wrap it in a case and store it away? Or do I seek a good price for it and sell it? The Master said, Sell it! Sell it! I myself await an offer. (9.13)

[Zigong, knowing that the Master possesses the Way but has not been given the opportunity to put it into practice in an official capacity, poses the two alternatives. The Master definitely would prefer to sell, that is, to attempt to put his Way into practice.]

54.   The Master wished to settle among the nine barbarian tribes in the east. Someone said, But what about their crudeness? The

---

8 Commentators agree that the *wu* 毋 here meaning "do not" should be read as *wu* 無 ("to be without").

Master said, If a superior man were to settle among them, there would be no crudeness. (9.14)

[The Master's words speak to the powerfully transforming effect that a morally upright person has on those around him—even on so-called barbarians.]

55.   The Master, standing by the side of a stream, said, It flows on and on like this, never stopping, day or night. (9.17)

[According to Zhu Xi the river exemplifies the unceasing activity of heaven and earth. Confucius intends his observation here as an exhortation to students: like the uninterrupted flowing of the stream, efforts at pursuing the Way must never come to an end.]

56.   The Master said, I have yet to meet a person who loves virtue as much as he loves beautiful women. (9.18)

57.   The Master said, The young should be held in awe. How do we know that in the future they will not be the equals of us today? If, however, at the age of forty or fifty they have not distinguished themselves, then indeed they do not deserve to be held in awe. (9.23)

[The young who choose to dedicate themselves to learning may, with time and effort, achieve great things. This passage serves to exhort people to give themselves entirely to the learning process. It also reminds the reader that most people are not born with an innate knowledge that distinguishes their behavior early on from that of others; distinguished behavior normally comes only with accumulated efforts, that is, with years of learning.]

58.   Make being true to yourself and true to others your guiding rule. Do not befriend those unlike you. And when you err, do not be afraid to correct yourself. (9.25)

59.   The Master said, The wise are not misled; the truly good are not anxious; the courageous are not afraid. (9.29)

[Neo-Confucians understand this passage in terms of Song metaphysics. "Brilliance can illumine principle and thus they will not be misled; principle can subdue selfishness and thus they will not be anxious; *qi* can adapt itself to what is moral and right, and thus they are not afraid. This is the sequence of learning." That is, only the wise person can become truly good and only the truly good person can become genuinely courageous.]

60.   If a mat was not straight he would not sit on it. (10.7)

[This and the next couple of analects reflect the profound importance of ritual, in its minutest detail, for Confucius. They also, according to Zhu's reading, reflect the intimate connection that Confucius posits between mind and body: in its physical expression the body reflects one's state of mind; at the same time the physical gestures and motions of the body help shape the state of mind. Thus, sitting on a mat that is straight is an expression of the Sage's mental correctness—even as the sitting promotes a perfectly balanced mind, free of distractions and biases.

Earlier commentators had simply explained that sitting on a mat that was straight is what proper ritual required. Thinkers of the Song and later gave considerably more attention to the internal springs of proper behavior.

This passage is a clear example of how Zhu would reconcile traditional teachings with the philosophical concerns and language of his day.]

61.   When a friend died but had no kin to whom the body could be entrusted, he [the Master] would say, It falls to me to care for his burial. On receiving a gift from a friend, even something as extravagant as a carriage and horses, he would not prostrate himself—unless it was sacrificial meat. (10.16)

[This speaks of the proper rites between friends. As for gifts, the commentary notes, they were material exchanges and did not in general require the recipient to prostrate himself, no matter how lavish the gifts were. But when presented with meat prepared for ancestral sacrifice

Confucius would bow to express respect for the friend's ancestors, just as he would for his own.]

62. When climbing into a carriage he would always stand up straight and grab the mounting strap. Once inside the carriage, he would not glance about, speak with haste, or point with his hand. (10.19)

63. The Master said, Hui! He is a person of no help to me. He finds nothing in my words that displeases him. (11.4)

[Although the remark may appear to express irritation with Yan Hui, great praise is intended, according to the commentary. The fact is that the moment Hui hears the Master's words, his mind-and-heart silently and fully comprehends them.]

64. Yan Yuan [Yan Hui] died. The Master said, Ah! Heaven has ruined me. Heaven has ruined me. (11.9)

[Heaven has deprived the Master of the disciple most capable of transmitting his Way. His special affection for Yan Hui is clear.]

65. Jilu [the disciple Zilu] asked about serving the spirits. The Master said, Unable to serve man, how are we able to serve the spirits? He then ventured to ask about death. The Master said, Not understanding life, how can we understand death? (11.12)

[The questions posed by Zilu are not unimportant, and Confucius is not avoiding them. For Neo-Confucians this passage does not—as it does for so many interpreters of the *Analects*—reflect a lack of interest in the spirit world, or agnosticism, as scholars often argue, but rather a commitment to the proper sequence of learning. Zhu writes, "Dead and living, beginning and end, initially are not of two principles. It is simply that there is order to learning, which must be followed." Master Cheng comments that "the Way of understanding the living is the Way of understanding the dead; the Way of serving man to the utmost is the Way of serving the spirits to the utmost. Dead and living, man and spirits, are one and yet two, two and yet one."]

66.   Zigong asked, Who is more worthy, Shi or Shang? The Master said, Shi goes too far and Shang not far enough. He said, In that case isn't Shi superior? The Master said, Going too far is the same as not going far enough. (11.16)

[The disciples Zizhang (Shi) and Zixia (Shang) have both failed: Zizhang because he is impetuous, and Zixia because he is too cautious. Each of us must strive to achieve the perfect balance in whatever set of circumstances we find ourselves. This is the major theme of the last of the Four Books, *Maintaining Perfect Balance*.]

67.   Zilu asked about immediately putting into practice what one hears. The Master said, You have a father and older brother to consider. How can you immediately put into practice what you hear? Ranyu asked about immediately putting into practice what one hears. The Master said, Immediately put into practice what you hear. Gongxi Hua said, When Yu asked about immediately putting into practice what one hears, the Master said, You have a father and older brother to consider. When Qiu asked about immediately putting into practice what one hears, the Master said, Immediately put into practice what you hear. Now, I, Chi, am confused and dare to ask. The Master said, Qiu holds himself back, so I urged him on; Yu has the energy of two, so I held him back. (11.20)

[This passage picks up the theme of the previous one: Zilu goes too far and Ranyu not far enough. For this reason, the Master holds one back and urges the other on, hoping that each will weigh circumstances and act accordingly.

The exchange here also illustrates Confucius' mode of teaching. In instructing pupils, he resists offering up abstract principles; rather, he teaches to the individual, that is, he assesses the particular audience and answers accordingly. Thus, here are two quite different answers to the same question. This "perspectival" approach of the *Analects* explains in part why answers to questions about matters such as wisdom, true goodness, courage, and official service often differ from passage to passage.]

68. Yan Yuan asked about true goodness. The Master said, To subdue the self and return to ritual constitutes true goodness. If only for a single day someone subdues the self and returns to ritual, all under heaven will recognize his true goodness. The practice of true goodness rests with oneself, not with others. Yan Yuan said, I beg to know the details. The Master said, If contrary to ritual, do not look; if contrary to ritual, do not listen; if contrary to ritual, do not speak; if contrary to ritual, do not act. Yan Yuan said, Although I, Hui, am not clever, I beg to devote myself to these words. (12.1)

[Zhu Xi understood this passage differently from earlier Confucians. Since we are born with true goodness, as part of our heavenly endowed human nature, the challenge for each of us is to return to it, to give it full expression in daily life. The problem, of course, is that our allotment of psychophysical stuff, if not cultivated or refined, can easily lead us away from our goodness and in the direction of selfishness. For Zhu, and later Confucians, subduing the self in this passage means to subdue our selfish desires so that we can manifest the true goodness that is within. For them, again in contrast to earlier Confucians, in consequence of eliminating selfish desires one will accord entirely with ritual in all matters. Earlier interpreters took the passage to mean that the practice of ritual was a means by which to restrain the self from behaving badly.]

69. Zigong asked about government. The Master said, Let food be sufficient, let military preparations be sufficient, and let the people have faith in you. Zigong said, If you have absolutely no choice but to give up one of the three, which should go first? He said, Let the military preparations go. Zigong said, If you have absolutely no choice but to give up one of the remaining two, which should go first? Let the food go first. Since ancient times, nobody has escaped death. The people, without faith, have nothing on which to stand. (12.7)

[Without food the people will die, but death is unavoidable anyway. Without faith, though alive, the people will have nothing to sustain them. The ruler himself would prefer death to giving up the faith of the people; in turn, the people would prefer death to giving up faith in him.

That "military preparations" ranks last here anticipates what will become the traditional Confucian devaluation of military service and martial skill.]

70.   Duke Jing of Qi asked Confucius about governing. Confucius responded, Let the ruler be a ruler, the minister a minister, the father a father, and the son a son. The Duke said, Very good indeed! Truly, if the ruler is not a ruler, the minister not a minister, the father not a father, and the son not a son, even though there be sufficient grain, would I get to eat it? (12.11)

[When people act in all of their social roles as they ideally should, order and harmony result. With social order and harmony comes the security of the ruler.

This passage indicates the importance of the rectification of names (*zhengming* 正名) for the Master, the idea that only when terms reflect their reality are they meaningful. That is, a minister can be called a minister only when he behaves in a manner befitting a true minister.]

71.   In hearing lawsuits I am just like others. What is necessary is to see that there are no lawsuits. (12.13)

[Zilu, Confucius' disciple, and others do not appreciate that should a government rely on ritual and humility its people will not resort to lawsuits.]

72.   The superior man promotes the good in others, not the bad. The small person does the opposite. (12.16)

73.   Ji Kangzi [de facto ruler of Lu from 492–468 BCE] asked Confucius about governing. Confucius responded, To govern (*zheng* 政) means to correct (*zheng* 正). If you lead by correcting yourself, who would dare to remain incorrect? (12.17)

[As in #6, where the ruler is likened to the pole star, this analect speaks to the power of the ruler's moral example. So powerful is his moral example that to govern requires nothing more than rectifying himself. The characters for the two instances of *zheng* are orthographically distinct but homophonous.]

74.   Ji Kangzi asked Confucius about government, saying, Suppose I were to kill the Way-less in order to promote those possessed of the Way. What would you say? Confucius responded, You are governing; what need is there for killing? If you desire good, the people will be good. The virtue of the superior man is wind; the virtue of the small person is grass. When wind passes over it, the grass is sure to bend. (12.19)

[The grass/wind metaphor for the moral force exercised by the superior man over others is one of the most famous in the text and, indeed, in the classical tradition. Like #6, #7, and #73, this passage idealizes the situation of a ruler and government in which force need not be employed. It is important to note that the thrust of all of these passages is not simply that moral example provides social order, but that it brings about reform and correction in the people. In short, moral leadership ideally leads to the moral transformation of the subjects.

Despite the insistence that there be no use of force, the authoritarian implications of such remarks for later Chinese society may be evident. For, if people assume correctness and moral authority on the part of the ruler—simply by dint of his being the ruler—they readily assume a responsibility to accord with his actions and wishes, whatever they might be.]

75.   Zilu said, If the ruler of Wei were awaiting your services in government, what would you do first? The Master said, It most certainly would be the rectification of names. Zilu said, Is that right? How impractical you are. Why this rectification? The Master said, How crude you are, Yu. The superior man, when it comes to matters he does not understand, should offer no opinion.

If names are not rectified, words will not agree with reality; if words do not agree, then affairs will not result in success. If affairs do not result in success, then rites and music will not prosper; if rites and music do not prosper, then punishments will not be correct; if punishments are not correct, then the people will have no place to put hand or foot. Therefore, as to the superior man—when he names something it is sure to be sayable, and when he says something it is sure to be practicable. With respect to words the superior man is not careless in the slightest. (13.3)

[Reality and words must accord. Order depends on it. This explains why the rectification of names (*zhengming*) would be the first item of business for Confucius were he to be given the responsibility of governing. Zilu clearly is surprised and perplexed by the Master's response to his opening question, thus the Master's elaboration.]

76.   The Master said, If his person is correct, without his giving orders they will be carried out; if his person is not correct, though he gives orders they will not be obeyed. (13.6)

[The subject is clearly the ruler. The Master is once again speaking of the power of the morally charismatic leader.]

77.   The Master said, If there were someone to employ me, in the course of but twelve months, we would be doing well, and within three years, we would achieve success. (13.10)

[Confucius again registers his profound desire to hold office; his profound regret that no one acknowledges him; and his profound confidence that through him government could successfully transform the people.]

78.   The Duke of She asked about government. The Master said, The near are pleased and the distant approach. (13.16)

[Feeling the benefits of good government, those nearby are happy; those at a distance, hearing of the benefits, move closer in order to participate in them. Virtue attracts.]

79. The Duke of She spoke with Confucius, saying, In our community there was a certain "Mr. Upright." When his father stole a sheep, the son gave evidence against him. Confucius said, In our community the upright are different from this. A father covers up for his son and a son covers up for his father. This is where uprightness is to be found. (13.18)

[Zhu Xi comments that the covering up that a father and son do for each other is the "apex of heavenly principle and human emotion." He goes on to cite an earlier Song thinker, Xie Liangzuo (1050–1103), who had remarked that "to accord with principle constitutes uprightness" and then asked whether turning on one's own son or one's own father could possibly be consistent with principle.

It is such references to the metaphysical language of the Song that distinguishes Neo-Confucian readings—and the reading of the *Analects* by late imperial examination candidates—from earlier readings of the text.]

80. Fan Chi asked about true goodness. The Master said, At home be respectful; in managing affairs be attentive; with others do the best you can. Even though you go to dwell among the Yi or Di barbarians, you must not abandon these qualities. (13.19)

[The commentary distinguishes between being "respectful" (*gong* 恭) and being "attentive" (*jing* 敬). "Respect" manifests itself toward others, in a person's outward demeanor. "Attentiveness" is the mental seriousness and concentration a person brings to the task at hand; it is more an internal state.

Note here that, asked about true goodness, Confucius again presents characteristics or qualities of it, not a definition. These qualities are universally desirable, according to him, and are to be exhibited even when the truly good person finds himself among peoples who have no stake in Chinese culture or customs.]

81. The Master said, To be resolute and firm, simple and slow in speech, is to approach true goodness. (13.27)

[A person who is resolute and firm will "not give in to creaturely desires," which means that the goodness within will manifest itself more readily. The passage is explained in terms of the Song view that within each of us a battle wages between human emotions and human nature. If emotions become excessive and we fall prey to human desire, they will prevail over and obscure our good nature—as explained by Zhu in his comments on #1 of the *Great Learning*.]

82. The Master said, The superior man reaches high; the small person reaches low. (14.23)

[The superior man accords with heavenly principle, whereas the small person follows creaturely desires and thus sinks ever and ever lower. Again, the language of principle, human nature, and desires is used to explain a remark by the Master.]

83. The Master said, In ancient times, those who learned did so for the sake of themselves; nowadays those who learn do so for the sake of others. (14.24)

[Learning is about cultivating the self. It is not about impressing others; it is not about winning fame and recognition; and, for Zhu Xi, it is certainly not for the purpose of succeeding in the civil service examinations. Learning is about behaving well—authentically well— in all situations in life. In short, it is learning to be moral, for one's own sake.]

84. The Master said, The superior man is ashamed lest his words surpass his deeds. (14.27)

85. The Master said, The Ji horse was not praised for its strength but for its good character. (14.33)

[This, of course, is still truer of human beings.]

86. The Master said, Alas, no one knows me! Zigong said, Why is it that no one knows you? The Master said, I do not blame heaven

nor do I fault man. I study low to reach high—it must be heaven that knows me. (14.35)

[The Master again expresses disappointment that his abilities have not been recognized by the rulers of the day. But since he has spent his life devoted to self-cultivation, perhaps his commitment and achievements have been recognized above. To study low and reach high, according to the commentary, is "to study the affairs of man below in order to reach heavenly principle above." Studying is, therefore, about the successful investigation of things advocated in the text of the *Great Learning*.]

87.   The Master was playing the stone chimes in Wei. A man with a straw basket passed by Confucius' gate and said, With such a determined mind-and-heart does he play the stone chimes! After a little while, he said, How inelegant! How stubborn! If no one knows you, give it up: "If it is deep, let your robes drag in the water; if it is shallow, raise them up." [ode #34.][9] The Master said, What resolve! Nothing is difficult for him! (14.39)

[The passerby is a recluse, one who has chosen to withdraw physically from the entanglements of contemporary society; he represents a contemporary—perhaps a Daoist—alternative to the Confucian commitment to engage the social and political problems of the day. In the continual beating of the chimes, the recluse senses the heart of a person determined to follow his course, no matter the circumstances, a person desperate to serve in office. Confucius' final remark, in turn, is sarcastic, expressing impatience with the recluse, who, from the Master's point of view, is determined to follow the easiest, most convenient path. Never does he take on responsibilities that could possibly be of trouble to him.

The citation here is from the *Book of Odes* and indicates that the recluse is a person of some education who has made a choice to retire, not some rustic, uneducated peasant.]

---

9   Translation based on James Legge, *The Chinese Classics*, Vol. 4, p. 53.

88. Zilu asked about the superior man. The Master said, He cultivates himself so as to become fully attentive. Zilu said, This and nothing more? The Master said, He cultivates himself so as to ease the lot of others. Zilu said, This and nothing more? The Master said, He cultivates himself so as to ease the lot of all people. Even Yao and Shun would have found this difficult. (14.42)

["He cultivates himself so as to become fully attentive" says it all, perfectly and exhaustively, according to Zhu's commentary. But Zilu apparently does not get the full implications of the remark. Thus Confucius lays them out. A person engages in the self-cultivation process in order to perfect himself. But, naturally, self-cultivation goes beyond the self-perfection of the individual; it involves, too, extending one's self to others, feeling empathy for them, and doing the best one can to better their lives.]

89.   Duke Ling of Wei asked Confucius about going into battle. The Master responded, With matters of ritual, I am familiar; but never have I learned about matters of war. The next day he departed. In Chen, provisions ran out; his followers became so ill that none was able to pick himself up. Zilu, visibly displeased, said, Does even the superior man find himself in straitened circumstances? The Master said, The superior man remains firm in straitened circumstances, but the small person acts with abandon in straitened circumstances. (15.1)

[Ruling by military might does not accord with the Way, so the Master left Wei. In Chen, he explained that everyone confronts hardship, but the superior man in such circumstances behaves very differently from the small person.]

90. The Master said, Ruling through inactivity, is this not Shun! For what did he do? Assuming a reverential pose, he faced due south and nothing more. (15.5)

[Shun, through his abundant virtue, ruled effortlessly, bringing about the moral transformation of the people. By commenting here that Shun filled government posts with capable men and thus "left no traces of his activity behind," Zhu wished to distinguish Shun's *wuwei* 無為, or inactivity, from that of Daoist inactivity. Daoists, because of their belief that the world and the multitude of things spontaneously accord with a natural order, did not advocate for active government. Social harmony could be achieved of its own, without any need for direction from above. Thus, for them, the best government, if any were necessary at all, was inactive—a laissez-faire government. Shun's government, by contrast, was active indeed, the Neo-Confucians sought to emphasize here. It is simply that the presence of able ministers, chosen wisely by Shun, made action of his own unnecessary.]

91. The Master said, Not to talk with one who can be talked with is to waste a person; to talk with one who cannot be talked with is to waste words. A wise person does not waste people, neither does he waste words. (15.8)

92. The Master said, The superior man is distressed by his own inability, not by others not knowing him. (15.19)

[This passage reminds the reader that learning should be for the sake of oneself, not to impress others.]

93. The Master said, The superior man seeks it within himself; the small person seeks it within others. (15.21)

[The superior man's sense of worth comes from within; it is not something affirmed by recognition or praise by others.]

94. Zigong asked, Is there one word that can be practiced for the whole of one's life? The Master said, That would be "empathy" perhaps: what you do not wish yourself do not do unto others. (15.24)

[The aim of learning is moral perfection, which finds its expression in the unfailingly empathetic treatment of others. The word "empathy" (*shu*) is sometimes translated as "consideration for others" or "reciprocity" and means, according to Song Neo-Confucians, to treat others as one would wish to be treated oneself; it refers to an ability to put oneself in the place of others, to gauge the feelings of others using one's own as the standard. See #19 and #34.]

95.   The Master said, Man is capable of broadening the Way; it is not the Way that broadens man. (15.29)

[Man has consciousness whereas the Way is inactive. It is thus man that must will or set his mind on putting the Way into practice.]

96.   The Master said, Erring and not reforming: this indeed is what is meant by erring! (15.30)

[Constant attentiveness to one's own actions and the willingness to reform oneself are characteristics essential to becoming a superior man.]

97.   The Master said, Once I did not eat for the entire day or sleep for the entire night in order to think. It was of no use. Better to learn. (15.31)

[In pursuing the Way nothing is more important than fixing the will on learning. Learning results in knowledge, on the basis of which thinking and reflecting can be productive. This is intended as an exhortation to the disciples to commit to genuine learning.]

98.   The Master said, True goodness is more essential to the people than water and fire. I have seen people who have died by treading on water and fire; never have I seen a person die treading the path of true goodness. (15.35)

[Water and fire are things external to us that can do injury to a person's body. True goodness is internal; to give it up, even for a day, is to abandon our original mind-and-heart. Even worse, water and fire can sometimes kill, but true goodness never kills.]

99. The Master said, With instruction, there will be no distinctions. (15.39)

[This passage is explained by Zhu in terms of the contemporary metaphysics of human nature and psychophysical stuff. People are all born with the same good human nature but with different allotments of psychophysical stuff. With instruction, however, we are all—each and every one of us—capable of refining that stuff and returning to our original goodness.]

100. Those born knowing it are the highest, those who through learning come to know it are next, those who learn it but with difficulty are next, and those who because of difficulty do not learn it, these people are the lowest. (16.9)

[The reason for these differences, according to Neo-Confucians, is that people have different endowments of psychophysical stuff.]

101. The Master said, By nature near together, in practice far apart. (17.2)

[It is worth quoting Zhu's commentary here because it demonstrates vividly how Neo-Confucians brought their worldview to their reading of the *Analects*, thereby changing how the text would be understood by later generations; it also illustrates neatly the metaphysical grounding they gave to the teachings of the Master: "What is called nature here is spoken of in combination with the psychophysical stuff. In the psychophysical nature there are indeed differences of excellent and bad. Still, if we speak of the very beginning, people's natures are not very far apart at all. It is just that people practice good and so become good, or practice bad and so become bad. Only thus do they grow far apart."]

102. The Master said, Only the most wise and most stupid do not change. (17.3)

[The commentary ties the reading of this passage to the previous one, saying that even given the similarity in the psychophysical nature of people, some people's *qi* is so fixed in its good or bad quality that despite habitual practice it cannot be changed. Most people's stuff, of course, is malleable, and thus the sentiments found in #100.]

103.   The Master said, "Ritual, ritual": does it mean nothing more than jade and silk? "Music, music": does it mean nothing more than bells and drums? (17.9)

[As we have seen in earlier passages, ritual and music, to have any real meaning, must be sustained by inner feelings of reverence and harmony.]

104.   The Master said, I wish to give up speech. Zigong said, If you, our Master, were not to speak, what would we, your disciples, transmit? The Master said, Does heaven speak? From it the four seasons take their course; from it the hundred things receive life. Does heaven speak? (17.17)

[The cycle of seasons and the production of the myriad things are simply the expression of heavenly principle, which manifests itself and spreads everywhere; that is, the seasons and the production of things do not come about as a result of speech. The Sage, in motion and at rest, is the expression of the sublime Way and pure righteousness; this too is a matter of heavenly principle and happens without speech. The point here is that the Way of the Sage is luminous and evident of its own, observable in all that he does. Speech is unnecessary.]

105.   The Madman from Chu, Jieyu, went past Confucius, singing:

> Phoenix, Phoenix!
> How your virtue has decayed.
> For the past, there can be no reproach.
> But the future can still be salvaged.
> Stop! Stop!
> Those who nowadays take up office are in peril.

Confucius descended from his carriage hoping to speak with him, but he hastened his step and fled. He did not get to speak with him. (18.5)

[The Madman of Chu, drawing on the legend that the phoenix appears when the Way prevails and conceals himself when it does not, criticizes Confucius for his past inability to conceal himself and urges him to give up his hope for office in this time of trouble—as the Madman himself has done. Zhu's commentary observes that the Madman here is pointedly mocking the Master for ignoring his own advice, offered in #48: "When the Way prevails under heaven, show yourself; when the Way does not prevail, remain hidden."

Neo-Confucians attempt to defend the Master here by saying that the Madman flees because he knows the Master's views on when to take up office are right and does not wish to hear them. In my view, however, there is an unresolved tension in the *Analects*: on the one hand the Master opines often that when the Way is not evident in society and government, one has little choice but to withdraw and remain true to one's principles; at the same time the Master in his behavior and his words suggests throughout the text that the right person, with the right moral principles, has the wherewithal to reform government and society and guide them along the true path, the Way.

The Madman of Chu, whatever his reason for fleeing, represents a contemporary reclusive alternative to the Confucian expectation to serve and to better society; better, in his mind, to retire from this world and preserve oneself rather than to try to change it.]

106.   Chang Ju and Jie Ni were ploughing the field side by side. When Confucius passed their way, he had Zilu go ask them where the river crossing was. Chang Ju said, Who is holding the reins to the carriage? Zilu said, It is Kong Qiu. He said, Kong Qiu of Lu? Yes, he said. Chang Ju said, Then he knows where the crossing is. Zilu now asked Jie Ni. Jie Ni said, Who are you? He said, I am Zhong You. Jie Ni said, The disciple of Kong Qiu of Lu? Yes, he replied. He said, Flowing on and on, such is all under heaven. With whom can you change it? Now, wouldn't it be far better to follow a gentleman who flees from the world than one who flees from this man or that man? He then went on covering the seed without stopping. Zilu went to report to him, and the Master, perturbed, said, Flocking together with birds and beasts is impossible. If I were not to associate with followers of men, with whom would I associate? If

the Way prevailed under heaven, I, Qiu, would not be concerned with changing it. (18.6)

[This is another passage where recluses who have turned their backs on the world ridicule the Master for thinking he can reform it. In their view, best to flee from the world altogether. Compare with #87.]

107. Zixia [a prominent disciple known for his dedication to book learning] said, He who day to day recognizes where he is lacking, and month to month forgets not where he is capable, can be said to be fond of learning indeed. (19.5)

108. Zixia said, To be broad in learning and resolute in will; to question unyieldingly and reflect on what is near at hand: true goodness can be found therein. (19.6)

[The commentary stresses here that these four things do not constitute the practice of true goodness, but rather are the basis for the practice of true goodness. It is for that reason that the Master says, "true goodness can be found therein."]

109. Zixia said, The mistakes of the small person are always glossed over. (19.8)

[The small person avoids correcting his mistakes and would prefer to conceal them. See the contrast with the superior man in the following passage.]

110. Zigong said, The mistakes of the superior man are like the eclipses of the sun and moon. When he makes a mistake, everyone sees it. When he corrects it, everyone looks up to him. (19.21)

[The superior man can make mistakes. But rather than hiding them, he corrects them. For this he is admired all the more. The contrast with the small person in #109 is sharp.]

111. The Master said, Without an understanding of fate he has no way of becoming a superior man; without an understanding of ritual he has no way to take a stand; without an understanding of words he has no way to understand people. (20.3)

[Zhu Xi remarks that he who does not understand fate (*ming* 命) will flee from what will do him harm and hasten after what will profit him; he who does not understand ritual will be ill at ease; he who does not genuinely understand a person's words will not recognize whether the person is upright or not.]

The *Mencius*

THE MENCIUS[10] 孟子

1. Mencius went to see King Hui of Liang. The king said, "Sir. You've come here with little concern for the thousand *li* (approximately one-sixth of a mile). Surely you've brought something that will be of profit to my state?" Mencius responded, "Why must Your Majesty use the word 'profit'? Surely, it is true goodness and righteousness alone that matter. If the king were to say, 'What will be of profit to my state?' and the high officials were to say, 'What will be of profit to my family?' and gentlemen and commoners were to say, 'What will be of profit to myself?' everyone above and below would turn to attacking one another for profit and the state thereby would be put in grave danger. If the ruler of a state of ten thousand chariots were killed, it would be sure to be by someone from a thousand chariot state; and, if the ruler of a state of a thousand chariots were killed, it would be sure to be by someone from a family of one hundred chariots. To take a thousand from ten thousand or one hundred from one thousand can hardly be considered a little, yet those who put profit before righteousness are not satisfied until they seize it all. Never has a person given to true goodness abandoned those close to him; never has a person given to righteousness treated his lord as an afterthought. Let Your Majesty say, 'It is true goodness and righteousness alone that matter.' Why must Your Majesty use the word 'profit'?" (1A.1)

[In this opening passage of the text, Mencius picks up on a theme that has run throughout the previous two books, the *Great Learning* and the

---

10 The *Mencius* is a text in seven books, each divided into a Part A and a Part B, each of which in turn is subdivided into chapters. Thus, the notation 1A.1 refers to Book 1, Part A, Chapter 1.

Analects: The moral leadership of the ruler has a powerful effect. He sets the example for the people.

King Hui of Liang is roundly admonished by Mencius to speak not of profit but only of true goodness and righteousness. To speak of profit, he suggests, will prompt others to speak of and pursue profit, which surely will not benefit the king or his state. To speak of true goodness and righteousness will influence others to pursue true goodness and righteousness; in the end, it is the pursuit of these virtues by the king's people that will profit him and his state.]

2.   [In reply to a question from King Hui of Liang about government, Mencius responds:]

"Do not interfere with the farming seasons and the crops will be more than can be consumed; do not let finely meshed nets be cast in ponds and lakes and the fish and turtles will be more than can be consumed; let axes enter the mountain groves only at the appropriate time and the timber will be more than can be used. When crops and fish and turtles are more than can be consumed, and timber is more than can be used, the people will nurture the living and mourn the dead in contentment. Their nurturing of the living and the mourning of the dead in contentment: such is the beginning of the kingly way. Let mulberry trees be planted in households of five *mu* (approximately one-sixth of an acre) and fifty-year-olds can wear silk; do not let the times for breeding chickens, pigs, dogs, and hogs be neglected, and the seventy-year-olds can eat meat. In fields of one hundred *mu*, do not deprive them of the seasons, and families of several mouths will never go hungry. Be attentive to instruction in the village schools and set forth the principles of filial piety, and fraternal respect and those with graying hair will not be on the roads carrying heavy loads on their backs and heads. It is impossible in a state where seventy-year-olds wear silk and eat meat, and the black-haired people suffer from neither hunger nor cold, for the ruler not to be regarded as a true king. If pigs and hogs eat the food meant for the people and you know not how to restrain them, and if there are famished dying on the roads and you know not how to distribute aid from the granaries and then say, 'It is not me; it is just a bad year,' how is this any different from mutilating and killing a

person and then saying, 'It is not me; it is the weaponry.' Let the
king not put blame on a bad year and all under heaven will come to
him." (1A.3)

[What is interesting about this passage is the concrete nature of Mencius'
suggestions for what makes for good government. Confucius, of course,
urged that the government be good and that it treat the people well,
with consideration for their welfare. But Mencius goes much further
here: he tells the reader, in rather prescriptive terms, what precisely is
meant by good government and treating the people. Mencius believes
that a true ruler must provide for the material needs of the people; this
is the beginning of the kingly way for it is the means of winning their
mind-and-hearts. Master Cheng, in Zhu's commentary, remarks that
Mencius' theory of the kingly way is this and nothing more and describes
it as "concrete."]

3.   [In response to a question from King Hui of Liang about government, Mencius responds:]
    "Even with only one hundred square *li* of land one can become a
true king. If Your Majesty carries out truly good government among
the people, is sparing in the use of punishment, taxes lightly, and gets
people to plough deeply and keep control of the weeds, then the able-
bodied, in their leisure time, will practice filial piety and fraternal
respect, keep true to themselves and true to their word, within the
home serve their fathers and elder brothers, outside the home serve
their elders and superiors, and thus can be made, with sticks alone,
to strike Qin and Chu with their strong armor and sharp weaponry.
The enemy rulers deprive their people of the seasons so that they
cannot plough and weed and thereby care for their fathers and
mothers; fathers and mothers grow cold and famished while brothers, wives, and children scatter in all directions. They entrap and
drown their people. If Your Majesty should go and attack, whosoever
would side against you? For this reason, it is said, 'The truly good
has no enemies.' Your Majesty, I beg you, have no doubts." (1A.5)

[Mencius here prescribes still more concrete measures to be taken by a
good ruler. Should King Hui of Liang himself decide to take such

measures, he would win the devotion of his people. As a result, they would be quick to take up arms on his behalf, even against larger and stronger states; at the same time the people of these larger and stronger states would withdraw their support from their rulers and give it to him. Good government again triumphs and leads to a larger and stronger state. Passage 2A.5 is similar.]

4.   King Xuan of Qi asked, "May I hear about the affairs of Huan of Qi and Wen of Jin?" Mencius replied, "Disciples of Confucius did not speak of Huan or Wen and so nothing has come down to later generations. I know nothing of them. But do allow me to go on about the way of the true king." Xuan of Qi said, "What sort of virtue enables one to become a true king?" Mencius said, "To give protection to the people is to be a true king. No one would be able to resist." "Is someone like me able to give protection to the people?" "Yes." "How do you know I can?" "I have heard Hu He recount the following:

> While the king was sitting in the upper part of the temple hall someone led an ox through the lower part. Seeing this, the king said, "Where is the ox going?" "It will be slaughtered and its blood used to consecrate the new bell." The king said, "Let it go. I cannot bear to see it trembling in fear, like an innocent person being hauled off to the execution ground." "If so, are we to dispense with the consecration of the new bell?" "How can we dispense with that? Substitute a sheep for it."

"Did this really happen?" The king said, "Yes, it did." Mencius said, "One with such a mind-and-heart is capable of being a true king. The people all assumed Your Majesty to be stingy, but I certainly know that it was because Your Majesty could not bear to see the ox's suffering." The king said, "It was indeed the case that there were people who ridiculed me. But even though the state of Qi may be cramped, could I possibly have begrudged one ox? It was that I could not bear to see it trembling in fear, like an innocent person being hauled off to the execution ground, and so substituted a sheep for it." "Your Majesty mustn't think it strange that the people assumed you to be stingy, for you took the small and substituted it for the large. Why would they understand? If Your Majesty was pained that an innocent was being hauled off to the execution ground what is there to distinguish between an ox and a sheep?" The king laughed and said, "What, in fact, was on my mind? It was not that I begrudged the cost of the ox—and yet I did substitute it with a sheep. It makes sense that the people took me to be stingy." "No harm's been done. What you did after all was practice the craft of true goodness: you had seen the ox but had not seen the sheep. The superior man relates to an animal thus: seeing it alive he cannot bear to see it dead; hearing the sound it makes he cannot bear to eat its flesh. This is the reason a superior man keeps his distance from the kitchen." Pleased, the king said, "The *Odes* say: 'What others have in their mind-and-hearts / I, with reflection, can gauge.' [From #198] This speaks of you. Now, it was I who did it and yet when I sought within, I could not grasp my own mind-and-heart. Now, you offer your words and my mind-and-heart is stirred. How is it that this mind-and-heart is equal to that of a true ruler?" "Suppose there is a man who tells you: 'Whereas my strength is sufficient to lift three thousand catties, it is not sufficient to lift a feather, and whereas my eyesight is sufficient to examine the tip of an autumn hair, it is not sufficient to see a cartload of wood.' Would Your Majesty grant what he had said?" "No." "Now when kindness is sufficient to reach animals but its benefits are not extended to the people, is this any different? Thus, when a feather is not lifted, it is because one does not exert strength; when a cartload of firewood is not seen, it is because one does not use one's eyesight. When the people are not given protection, it is because one does not employ kindness. Consequently, Your Majesty's not being a true king is a matter of your not doing it; it is not a matter of your being incapable." He said, "Is there any difference in form between 'not doing it' and 'being incapable'?" "To tell people 'I am incapable of taking Mount Tai underarm and leaping over the North Sea' is genuinely 'to be incapable'; to tell people 'I am incapable of breaking up branches for kindling at the request of an elder" is 'not doing it'—it is not 'to be incapable.' Thus, Your Majesty's not being a true king is not in the category of taking Mount Tai underarm and leaping over the North Sea. Your Majesty's not being a true king is in the category of breaking

up branches. Treat your own elders with the respect elders deserve
and then extend that treatment to the elders of others; care for your
own young and then extend that care to the young of others, and
all under heaven can be rolled in the palm of your hand. The *Book
of Odes* says:

> Serve as example for your wife
> Extend it further to your brothers
> And thereby manage family and state. [#240]

This means nothing more than to take this mind-and-heart of yours
and apply it to others. Thus, he who extends his bounty can preserve
all within the four seas; he who does not extend his bounty cannot
even preserve his own wife and children. It is in this regard and
nothing more that ancients far surpassed other men: they were good
at extending to others what they had done for themselves. At present
your bounty is sufficient to reach animals, but your benefits stop
short of reaching the people. Why is this so in your case alone?
Weigh it, and only then do we know whether it is light or heavy;
measure it, and only then do we know whether it is long or short.
This is true of all things, and most especially of the mind-and-heart.
Your Majesty, I beg you to take measure of yours. Is it only when
Your Majesty raises provisions for war, endangers soldiers and officers, and arouses the enmity of the various lords that your mind-
and-heart fills with joy?" "No. How could I take joy in these matters?
It is just that I want to fulfill my most cherished desire." "May I hear
what Your Majesty's most cherished desire is?" The king laughed
and did not speak a word." Mencius said, "Is it that the rich and
sweet foods are not sufficient to satisfy your mouth? Or that the
light and the warm clothing are not sufficient to satisfy your body?
Or that the beautifully colored things are not sufficient for your eyes
to gaze upon? Or that sounds and voices are not sufficient for your
ears to behold? Or that your servants are not sufficient to receive
your personal orders? Your Majesty's various ministers are capable
of seeing to all of these matters, so your cherished desire cannot
possibly be on their account." "No, it is not on their account." "Then
Your Majesty's most cherished desire may be known. Your desire is

to extend your territory, to bring Qin and Chu to your court to pay homage, to rule over the Middle Kingdom, and to pacify the barbarians on your four borders. To do what you have been doing in search of what you desire is like climbing a tree in search of fish." The king said, "Is it really all that bad?" "It is even worse. For, whereas climbing a tree in search of fish may not gain you a fish, neither will it lead to disaster. But in doing what you have been doing in search of what you desire, exhausting all of the resources of your mind-and-heart, disaster is sure to ensue." "May I hear more?" "If the people of Zou and the people of Chu were to go to war, who, Your Majesty, would win?" "The people of Chu would win." "Thus it is clear that the small cannot contend with the large, the few cannot contend with the many, and the weak cannot contend with the strong. The territory within the seas is made up of nine regions, each of one thousand square *li*. Qi [your state] makes up one of them. For one to try to subdue the other eight is no different from Zou contending with Chu. Best to turn back to the fundamentals. If Your Majesty were to establish a government that practices true goodness, under heaven, all servants of government would long to stand in Your Majesty's court; all farmers would long to farm in Your Majesty's uncultivated fields; all merchants, traveling and resident, would long to warehouse their goods in Your Majesty's markets; all travelers would long to use Your Majesty's roads; and all under heaven who long to express displeasure with their rulers would come to Your Majesty to complain. If this were all so, who would be capable of resisting?" The king said, "I am dull-witted and have been unable to advance to this point. I would like for you, sir, by way of assisting me in my ambitions to provide me with clear instruction. Although I am not clever, please do give it a try." He said, "To have a constant mind-and-heart without a constant livelihood is something that a gentleman alone is capable of. If the people lack a constant livelihood it follows that they will lack a constant mind-and-heart. And if they lack a constant mind-and-heart, they will become reckless and depraved and there is nothing they will not do. To lead them into crime and then follow it up with punishment is to deceive the people. Is it possible that a truly good man in a high position would deceive the people? For

this reason, an enlightened ruler supervises the livelihood of the
people, making sure that they can adequately serve their parents
above and care for their wives and children below, and that in good
years they are abundantly full and in bad years escape death. Only
afterward urge them on toward good. The people, as a consequence,
will be quick to follow you. Today, with your supervision of the
people's livelihood, they cannot adequately serve their parents
above, nor care for their wives and children below. In good years
they suffer, and in bad years they do not escape death. In this situation they simply protect themselves from death, fearful that they
will not have sufficient means. They have not the leisure to attend
to ritual and righteousness.

If Your Majesty wishes to practice good government why do you
not return to the basics? Let mulberry trees be planted in households of five *mu* and fifty-year-olds can wear silk; do not let the
times for breeding chickens, pigs, dogs, and hogs be neglected, and
the seventy-year-olds can eat meat. In fields of one hundred *mu*, do
not deprive them of the seasons, and families of several mouths will
never go hungry. Be attentive to instruction in the village schools
and set forth the principles of filial piety, and fraternal respect and
those with graying hair will not be on the roads carrying heavy
loads on their backs and heads. It is impossible in a state where the
elderly wear silk and eat meat, and the black-haired people suffer
from neither hunger nor cold, for the ruler not to be regarded as a
true king." (1A.7)

[This chapter is central to Mencius' system of thought. People are born
with the beginnings of goodness, he says throughout his writings, but
these beginnings must be allowed, even encouraged, to develop. This
is where the responsibility of the government comes in; it must provide
for the material well-being of the people if it hopes that people will
behave well, in accord with their innate nature. If people are desperate
about mere survival and the protection and security of their elderly and
their young, the practice of ritual and righteousness has very little
urgency for them. Indeed, they will regard ritual and righteousness as
mere luxuries.

Few passages in the text are as powerful as one in this chapter: "To have a constant mind-and-heart without a constant livelihood is something that a gentleman alone is capable of. If the people lack a constant livelihood it follows that they will lack a constant mind-and heart. And if they lack a constant mind-and-heart, they will become reckless and depraved and there is nothing they will not do. To lead them into crime and then follow it up with punishment is to deceive the people. Is it possible that a truly good man in a high position would deceive the people?"

Early in the chapter Mencius expresses befuddlement over King Hui of Liang's capacity to extend kindness and generosity toward animals but not toward people. This is to stand the proper order on its head. Normally, one proceeds from being truly good toward people to loving other creatures. It is the king's mind that is problematic here, Mencius concludes. Zhu explains in his commentary that the king's "mind-and-heart of loving other creatures is heavy and long, and his mind-and heart for being good to the people is light and short, which is to abandon the proper order. And he himself is not even aware of it."

This chapter, 1A.7, is, in my view, one of the most effective summaries of what Mencius sees as the responsibilities of government. The government that successfully carries them out is what he means by good government.]

5. Mencius said to King Xuan of Qi: "Suppose one of Your Majesty's ministers entrusts his wife and children to a friend and then takes leave to journey to Chu, only to find, upon his return, that his wife and children suffer from cold and famine: What should be done?" He said, "Break off the friendship." He said, "Suppose the chief judge proved incapable of managing the junior judges: What should be done?" The king said, "Remove him." Suppose that all within the four borders is not well governed: What should be done?" The king looked around to his left and to his right and then spoke of other matters. (1B.6)

[Mencius is setting King Xuan up here. Quick to know what should be done in the first two cases proposed by Mencius, the king seems unprepared for the third, which, in Mencius' view, follows logically and obviously from the first two. Mencius would have King Xuan reflect seriously about the responsibilities of the true king.]

6.   King Xuan of Qi asked, "Is it the case that Tang banished Jie and King Wu cut down Zhou?" Mencius responded, "So it says in the records." King Xuan said, "Is it permissible for a minister to murder his sovereign?" Mencius said, "A thief of true goodness is called 'thief'; a thief of righteousness is called 'criminal.' Thieves and criminals are called good-for-nothings. I have heard of the punishment of the good-for-nothing Zhou; I have not heard of the murder of a sovereign. (1B.8)

[This passage has rightly received a lot of attention over the centuries. First, it speaks to the Confucian concern with bringing reality into accord with names, that is, the rectification of names. See passage #75 of the *Analects*, for instance. A sovereign is to be called a sovereign only when he comports himself as a "true" sovereign should. Clearly, in Mencius' view, and in view of the long tradition preceding Mencius, neither Jie nor Zhou was worthy of the title "sovereign." Thus, killing Zhou was not a matter of regicide, but a matter of killing a good-for-nothing who had abandoned the proper way of a ruler. This leads to the more important point: Mencius is implying here that a sovereign who does not behave as a true sovereign may be deposed by his ministers. With this passage the ruler's responsibility to care for the welfare of the people is backed up by the threat of removal by force.]

7.   [The disciple Gongsun Qiu] said, "Might I ask if I could hear about your unstirrable mind-and-heart and Gaozi's unstirrable mind-and-heart?"[11] Mencius answered, "Gaozi says, 'Do not seek in the mind-and-heart what you fail to find in words; do not seek

---

11 Zhu understands the "unstirrable mind-and-heart" to be a mind-and-heart that is undistracted and unprejudiced, one that has reached the point where apprehensions and doubts no longer threaten its equilibrium.

in the *qi* what you fail to find in the mind-and-heart.'[12] That you do not seek in the *qi* what you fail to find in the mind-and-heart is fine, but that you do not seek in the mind-and-heart what you fail to find in words is not. The will is the commander of the *qi*, and the *qi* fills the body. The will comes first, and the *qi* follows. For this reason, I say, "Hold on to the will and do no violence to the *qi*." Gongsun Qiu said, "Having said that 'the will comes first and the *qi* follows,' why do you then go on to say, 'hold on to the will and do no violence to the *qi*'?" Mencius said, "The will, when concentrated, stirs the *qi*; the *qi*, when concentrated, stirs the will. Now, tumbling and hurrying belong to the *qi* and yet they stir our mind-and-heart."

"May I ask, sir, in what it is that you excel?" Mencius said, "I understand words. And I am good at nurturing my vast, flowing *qi*." Gongsun Qiu said, "May I ask what you mean by 'vast, flowing *qi*'?" Mencius said, "It is difficult to put in words. This *qi* could not be larger or more resolute. Nurture it with rectitude so that nothing brings harm to it and it will fill up the space between heaven and earth. This *qi* is partner of righteousness and the Way. Without it we become starved. It is born of accumulated righteousness; it is not attained through incidental acts of righteousness. If our actions do not satisfy the mind-and-heart, we become starved. Therefore I say, 'Gaozi does not know righteousness because he makes it something external to us.' We are bound to take action, but there must be no calculation associated with it. Our mind-and-heart must not lose sight of it, but neither must we assist in its growth. Don't be like the man from Song: There was a man from Song who was distressed that his shoots of corn were not growing and so he tugged at them. Wearily, he returned home and said, 'I have exhausted myself today; I have been helping the sprouts to grow.' His son hurried out to take a look; the sprouts had all withered. Under heaven, there are but a few who do not help the sprouts to grow. Some feel that they can be of no benefit at all and thus neglect the sprouts entirely; they are

---

[12] Gaozi is a philosophical rival of Mencius. He appears most prominently in Book 6.

the ones who don't even bother to weed. Some actively help in the growing process; these are the ones who pull at the sprouts. It is not just that they are of no benefit—they even do harm."

"What do you mean by 'understanding words'?" Mencius said, "In the case of a half-truth, to understand what it is concealing; in the case of seductive language, to understand the trap that it is setting; in the case of deceitful language, to understand the lies that are behind it; in the case of evasive language, to understand the desperation that motivates it. Produced in the mind-and-heart such language does injury to government, and what issues forth from government does injury to the conduct of affairs. When a sage again arises, he is certain to follow my words. . . ." (2A.2)

[This has long been regarded as a perplexing passage. Various commentators have struggled to make sense of it.

For Neo-Confucians, *qi* is the vital energy, the psychophysical stuff, that constitutes the entire universe and all things in it. Everything has its own particular endowment of this stuff. This *qi* that fills our body follows the lead of the mind-and-heart. In turn, the mind-and-heart is given its direction by the so-called will (*zhi* 志), which Zhu Xi glosses as "where the mind is headed." That is, if our will is inclined in the right direction, our vital psychophysical stuff follows. The source of "right" or "righteous" behavior, for Mencius, then, is internal, to be found in the mind-and heart—and the direction given it by the will— not external, as Gaozi[13] would have it. This, of course, explains why Mencius is concerned that we maintain firm control over our will, a theme emphasized earlier by Confucius. Indeed, in the Song, Zhu and his followers would make "establishing or fixing the will" one of their most common refrains. But, it is not only the will that moves the vital psychophysical stuff, according to Mencius; sometimes the stuff can move the will. This, again, explains why we must all the more firmly fix our will. In the commentary, however, Master Cheng is quick to add that only rarely does the psychophysical stuff stir the will; in 90

---

13 Gaozi holds an opposing view—that human nature is neither good nor evil, and that behavior is shaped by the environment.

percent of the cases it is the will that stirs and leads the psychophysical stuff.

Zhu reminds the reader that all of us of course are endowed with this vital stuff, and in all of us it is originally vast and flowing. But because we neglect it, that is, because we fail to nurture it, it becomes weak and famished. It is for this reason that Mencius urges us to nurture it with righteousness; through such nurturing we can return this psychophysical stuff to its original vital state. The impulse to nurture it, however, must be genuine, emanating naturally and without any calculation from the mind-and-heart within. And, as Master Cheng remarks in Zhu's commentary, since heaven and man are one, and no distinction is to be made between them, the vast, flowing psychophysical stuff of the universe is one with our vast, flowing psychophysical stuff; this being the case, if we nurture ours and let no harm come to it, it will merge naturally with the universal vital psychophysical stuff. Thus successfully nurturing our vast, flowing vital stuff brings about a perfect balance and harmony with the cosmos. The implications of this passage are moral, to be sure, but extend beyond, into the realm of the spiritual.

This passage further urges us to become good at understanding words. Drawing once again on metaphysical terminology of the Song, Zhu explains that it is only once we have given full realization to our own mind-and-heart and good nature that we can investigate the principle in any and all words in the universe and measure fairly their truth and merit. "Understanding words" means the capability of understanding the principle that inheres in them, which, in turn, depends on one's own previous moral development.]

8. All people have a mind-and-heart that cannot bear to see the suffering of others. Former kings had a mind-and-heart that could not bear to see the suffering of others and thus had governments that could not bear to see the suffering of others. Ruling all under heaven was as simple for them as rolling it in the palm of the hand. Here is why I say that all men have a mind-and-heart that cannot bear to see the suffering of others: Today, no matter the person, if he suddenly comes upon a young child about to fall into a well, his mind-and-heart fills with alarm and is moved to compassion. It is

not because he wishes to ingratiate himself with the parents of the young child; nor is it because he seeks renown among villagers and friends; nor is it because he would hate the bad reputation. From this we can see that to be without a mind-and-heart of compassion is not to be human; to be without a mind-and-heart that is ashamed of evil in oneself and hates it in others is not to be human; to be without a mind-and-heart of humility and deference is not to be human; to be without a mind-and-heart of right and wrong is not to be human. The mind-and-heart of compassion is the seed of benevolence; the mind-and-heart that is ashamed of evil in oneself and hates it in others is the seed of righteousness; the mind-and-heart of humility and deference is the seed of propriety; the mind-and-heart of right and wrong is the seed of wisdom. People have these four seeds just as they have the four limbs. To have these four seeds but to deny their potential in oneself is to rob from oneself. To deny their potential in the ruler is to rob from the ruler. All of us have these four seeds within us; if we know to develop and bring each to completion, it will be like a blaze catching fire or a spring finding a path. He who is able to bring them to completion is capable of preserving all within the four seas; he who doesn't complete them is incapable of caring for his parents. (2A.6)

[This is one of the most famous and most frequently cited passages in the whole of the *Mencius*.

Zhu explains that whereas all human beings are born with the mind-and-heart that cannot bear to see the suffering of others, our creaturely desires typically harm it. Thus, few preserve this mind-and-heart. Zhu's reading here is again informed by the philosophical belief that there wages in human beings a moral contest between human nature and creaturely desires. If the creaturely desires in the end win out, the goodness that inheres in our original nature will not become manifest. But whereas that nature may not become manifest, we never lose it either. This is clear, according to Mencius, from the simple fact that all of us, no matter what our moral status, instinctively respond in the same way—with alarm and compassion—when we see a child teetering on the edge of a well. Note a crucially important point in the passage that is easy to overlook: Mencius never says that all of us actually rush to save the child. Why not? Because there is that moment, between feeling the pity and alarm and rushing to the child's side, when our desires, selfish feelings, and calculations arise and becloud the mind-and-heart that cannot bear to see the suffering of others. What if we were to get hurt or fall into the well? What if we attempted a rescue and then got blamed for failing or, even worse, got accused ourselves of pushing the child into the well? What if the child was from a family with whom our family had been feuding for generations? It is such thoughts that inhibit us from acting on our good instincts. This explains why Mencius argues that we are born with only the seeds of true goodness, righteousness, propriety, and wisdom, and that these seeds must necessarily be developed and brought to completion. In the Neo-Confucian understanding, by bringing the seeds to completion we give realization to the four cardinal virtues that constitute our human nature and triumph over our creaturely desires.]

9.   [In response to a question from Duke Wen of Teng about the proper way to govern a state, Mencius said:]

"The way of the common people is this: Those with a constant livelihood will have a constant mind-and-heart. Those without a constant livelihood will not have a constant mind-and-heart. And if they lack a constant mind-and-heart, they will become reckless and depraved and there is nothing they will not do. To lead them into crime and then follow it up with punishment is to deceive the people. Is it possible that a truly good man in a high position would deceive the people? . . .

[Later, the Duke] sent [his minister] Bizhan to inquire about the well-field system. Mencius replied: "Your ruler wishes to practice truly good government. And he has carefully chosen to employ you in this matter. You must give it your best effort. Truly good government necessarily begins with setting boundaries [i.e., otherwise strong men will appropriate the land for themselves]. When boundaries are not properly set, the well-fields will be of different size and the grain for emoluments from them unequal. It is for this reason that cruel rulers and corrupt officers are invariably slow in setting boundaries. Once boundaries are properly set, the apportioning of fields and the regulating of emoluments can be handled with ease.

"Teng's territory is small. Still, there will be noblemen and there will be peasantry, for without noblemen there is no one to provide order for the peasantry and without the peasantry there is no one to provide sustenance for the noblemen. I would suggest that in the countryside, one-ninth of the land be made into public fields, to be worked cooperatively, and in the cities, that people pay taxes of 10 percent on their own. The highest officers on down should each have a 'sacred field' [the produce from which is to be used in sacrifices]; the sacred field is to be fifty *mu*. In a family of commoners, the land given to the additional males who have reached the age of sixteen is to be twenty-five *mu*. When burying the dead and changing residences, people are not to leave the village. If those working the same well-field stand by one another in all matters, assist one another in keeping watch, and sustain one another in times of illness, people will be affectionate toward one another and live in harmony.

A well-field is to be one *li* square and to consist of nine hundred *mu*. In its center is the public field; the eight families each have their own one hundred *mu*. Together they cultivate the public field, and only when they are done do they venture to tend their private affairs. It is this that distinguishes the peasantry.

This is its general outline. As to its adaptation, that is up to you and His Majesty. (3A.3)

[This is the first mention in Chinese texts of the so-called well-field system—which takes its name from the tic-tac-toe character *jing* 井, meaning "well," that resulted from the pictogram for eight equal squares surrounding a central square. And whereas Mencius suggests earlier in this chapter that the well-field system was first employed during the Shang period, there is little historical evidence to support this. Zhu, in his commentary, adds that although the system was introduced in the Shang, it is the Zhou version of it that is described here by Mencius; this too has little evidence to support it. This discussion of the well-field system is likely an idealization of past land practices by Mencius, meant primarily to be a model for adoption by rulers of the present.

This call for a well-field system follows logically and seamlessly from sentiments expressed earlier by Mencius. After all, if good government is to care for the material welfare of the people, then to care for the material welfare of people in an agrarian society is to ensure they have land. With a plot of land and its bounty, the people can hope to succor their parents above and their wives and children below. Knowing that the family is cared for, they will be less anxious and thus less prone to untoward behavior; they will also have the leisure to attend to rituals and righteousness (cf. Mencius, in #4).

The brief reference to occupational distinction between nobleman and peasant foreshadows Mencius' fuller discussion in the next passage, #10.]

10. There was one Xu Xing who spread the teachings of Shen Nong. Journeying to Teng from Chu, he proceeded directly to the gate and announced to Duke Wen, "A man from distant parts heard that you, Majesty, practice truly good government. He wishes to receive a place to live and become your unworthy subject." Duke Wen gave him a place. His followers, all several tens of them, wore coarse cloth, and made sandals and wove mats for a living.

Chen Liang's disciple, Chen Xiang, and his younger brother, Xin, carrying ploughs on their back journeyed from Song to Teng. They said, "We have heard that Your Majesty practices the government of the sages; that makes you a sage too. We wish to become subjects of a sage." When Chen Xiang met up with Xu Xing he was greatly pleased and, abandoning all that he had learned earlier, took to learning from him. When Chen Xiang met up with Mencius he conveyed the teachings of Xu Xing: "The ruler of Teng is a genuinely worthy ruler. Even so, he has not yet heard the Way. A worthy man plows for his food side by side with the people and cooks his own meals, even while he governs. Today, Teng has granaries and treasuries; this is to harm the people so that he might care for himself. Can he really be worthy then?"

Mencius said, "Is it that Master Xu must first plant grain before eating it?" "Yes." "Is it that Master Xu must first weave cloth garments before wearing them?" "No. He wears garments of coarse woolen cloth." "Does Master Xu wear a cap?" "Yes, he does." "What kind of cap?" "A simple, plain cap." "Does he weave it himself?" "No, he exchanges grain for it." "Why doesn't Master Xu do the weaving himself?" "It would be a detriment to his working the land." "Does Master Xu use a cauldron and steamer? Does he use iron ploughs and such?" "Yes." "Does he make them himself?" "No, he exchanges grain for them."

"To exchange grain for tools and implements imposes no hardship on potters and founders. And when potters and founders exchange tools and implements for grain, there just as surely is no hardship imposed on farmers. Now why doesn't Master Xu become a potter and founder and simply get everything he needs from his own house? Why does he go hither and thither to trade with the hundred craftsmen? Why does Master Xu not spare himself the trouble?" Chen said, "Surely the work of the hundred crafts cannot be done at the same time as ploughing."

"If that's so, is it ruling the empire alone that can be done at the same time as ploughing? There is the work of great men and the work of small men. Each person is provided for by the hundred craftsmen. If everyone were required to make everything he uses, the entire empire would be incessantly busy and have no time off. For this reason, it is said, 'Some labor with their mind-and-hearts; some labor with their strength. Those who labor with their mind-and-hearts govern others; those who labor with their strength are governed by others. Those who are governed provide for others; those who govern are provided for by others. This is a universally acknowledged principle. . . . ' "

Chen said, "If we follow the way of Master Xu, prices in the market will be fixed. There will be no dishonesty in the kingdom. Even though we send but a young boy to market, no one will cheat him. Cloth or silk of equal length will be the same price. Linen thread or silk wadding of equal weight will be the same price. Five grains of equal measure will be the same price. Shoes of equal size will be the same price."

Mencius said, "It is in the nature of those things to be unequal. Sometimes the discrepancy in value is onefold or fivefold, sometimes tenfold or one hundredfold, and sometimes one thousandfold or ten thousandfold. If you rank them equally, you throw the world into confusion. Suppose shoes, large and small, were the same price—who would make large ones? If we follow the way of Master

Xu, people would lead one another to the practice of dishonesty. Can we possibly govern a state this way?" (3A.4)

["Shen Nong" refers to the legendary "Divine Farmer" who is said to have taught people agriculture and to have invented the plough and hoe.

For Mencius good government is based on a well-field system that provides for the people. Chen Xiang, a recent "convert" to the teachings of Xu Xing, or Master Xu, zealously takes exception to it, arguing instead that only when the ruler works the land side by side with the people and cooks for himself, just as they do, can he be called worthy and good. The well-field system, in his view, creates strong status distinctions. Mencius counters that such distinctions are natural, even necessary, citing a passage from the tradition to support his position: "Some labor with their mind-and-hearts; some labor with their strength." Mencius believes that between them there is a fundamental reciprocity, just as there is between the farmer and the potter or founder. As Zhu Xi comments: "The sovereign without the small man suffers from hunger; the small man without the sovereign lives in chaos." This passage constitutes then a defense of a division of labor in society and a free market economy; differences in the quality of similar products should naturally be reflected in the difference between their prices, Mencius suggests. Indeed, Zhu concludes, the very inequality of things is a matter of natural principle (*li*).

The later tradition would often draw on this passage from the *Mencius* in offering a defense of hierarchy in Chinese society.]

11.   Gongduzi said, "Everyone outside your fold claims that you are fond of disputation. May I venture to ask why?" Mencius said, "It isn't that I'm fond of disputation; it's that I have no alternative. Heaven gave birth to the people long ago. At times order has prevailed, and at times disorder. . . .

"[These days] sage kings do not appear; the various lords do entirely as they wish; gentlemen out of office express intemperate views; and the doctrines of Yang Zhu and Mo Di fill the empire. In the empire those doctrines that cannot be traced back to Yang are surely traceable to Mo. The 'egoism' of Yang has no place for the

sovereign; the 'universal love' of Mo has no place for the father. To
have no place for a father or a sovereign is to be a beast. Gongming
Yi [a student of Confucius' disciples mentioned by Mencius in 3A.1]
said, 'When there is fleshy meat in the kitchen and plump horses in
the stable but the people here look famished and those in the countryside are starving: this is to lead beasts to feed on man.' When
the way of Yang and Mo does not stop and the Way of Confucius
is nowhere manifest: this is to delude the people with heresies and
obstruct the path of goodness and righteousness. To obstruct the
path of goodness and righteousness is to lead beasts to feed on man
and men to feed on one another. Fearful of this, I defend the Way
of our former sages against that of Yang and Mo and expel their
depraved expressions, so heresy cannot arise. For what arises in
the mind-and-heart does injury to the conduct of affairs, and what
arises from the conduct of affairs does injury to government. When
a sage next rises up, he will make no changes to these words of
mine.

"Long ago Yu quieted the flooding waters and the empire became
tranquil. The Duke of Zhou incorporated the barbarian tribes from
east and north and expelled the savage beasts, and the people were
at peace. Confucius completed the *Spring and Autumn Annals* and
rebellious subjects and wicked sons were filled with fear. The *Book
of Odes* says:

> He faces down the wild tribes from west and north,
> He punishes Jing and Shu.
> Thus no one dares take us on. [#300]

To have no place for fathers and no place for sovereigns is what the
Duke of Zhou attacked.

"I too wish to set the people's mind-and-heart in the right, to put
a stop to heresy, to keep wrong conduct at a distance, and to expel
depraved expressions, and, thereby, to carry on the work of the
three sages [i.e., Yao, the Duke of Zhou, Confucius]. It isn't that I'm
fond of disputation; it's that I have no alternative. He who is able
with words to repudiate Yang and Mo is a follower of the sages."
(3B.9)

[Yao, Shun, and Yu were the great and good emperors of China's legendary past; the Duke of Zhou, one of the founding fathers of the Zhou, has been regarded since the time of Confucius as the benevolent regent for the young King Cheng, largely responsible for the institutional innovations that, at least in Confucius' view, made the early Zhou an ideal society (cf. *Analects* #36).

Mencius presents himself here as a defender of the faith—at a time when the faith is in need of defending. Sages such as Yao, Shun, Yu, the Duke of Zhou, and Confucius had seen to it that the Way prevailed. But ever since the time of Confucius, the Way has been in decline and the world in decay. To resuscitate the Way of the sages, in Mencius' view, requires the repudiation of the popular teachings of the thinkers Yang Zhu (fl. fourth century BCE) and Mo Di (fl. fifth century BCE). Yang Zhu is associated with a doctrine that places value on preservation of the self and longevity; thus everything that one does is for the purpose of benefiting oneself so that one may comfortably live out one's life. In this doctrine, other people and indeed the empire itself matter little. Mo Di holds the view that if "universal love" were to prevail in the empire, fighting, disorder, and poverty would come to an end. But, the effect, according to Mencius and other Confucians, is that there would be no distinction between love for a father and love for a stranger. Consequently, the Confucian principle of graded affection, in which it is believed that the degree of love one feels toward another depends naturally on the closeness of the particular relationship, would be violated.

Scholars have argued that there in fact is little evidence to suggest that Yang Zhu's views had much currency at this time.[14] But his views do serve a rhetorical purpose. They allow Mencius to set up Yang and Mo as two extremes and to place the teachings of his beloved sages in the middle, as a perfect compromise between the two. Yang's "everyone for himself" theory ignores the responsibility that the individual owes to his ruler—and to those around him, whereas Mozi's idea of "universal love" ignores the natural primacy of the love a child feels for his

---

[14] E.g., Benjamin I. Schwartz, *The World of Thought in Ancient China*, pp. 259–260.

father.[15] Mencius takes it as his mission to rid the world of these two extremes and to call for the Way of the sages to reemerge. Only when the Way has reemerged will order once again prevail.

The commentary cites Master Cheng, who remarks that the views of Yang and Mo were considerably more dangerous than those of the legalist thinkers Shen Buhai (fl. fourth century BCE) and Han Feizi (fl. third century BCE); he then remarks that the views of Buddhists are even more dangerous than those of Yang and Mo. The reason is that their views "come close to principle" and thus easily confuse people. The implication is clear: The true Way is in desperate need of defense once again!]

12.   Mencius said, "The compass and the square bring to perfection the square and the circle. The sage brings to perfection human relations. If you wish to be a sovereign exhaust the way of a sovereign. If you wish to be a minister exhaust the way of a minister. In both of these matters do nothing more than model yourself on Yao and Shun. Not to serve your sovereign as Shun served Yao is not to respect your sovereign. Not to govern the people as Yao governed the people is to rob the people. Confucius said, 'There are two ways and nothing more: goodness and not goodness.' Should the cruelty toward his people be extreme, he will himself be murdered and his state destroyed. Should it not be extreme, his person will be in danger and his state weakened. He will be given the name You ('The Dark') or Li ('The Cruel') [as were two of the Zhou kings], and though his sons be filial and his grandsons caring, they will find it impossible, even over the course of a hundred generations, to change the designation given him. This is what is meant when the *Book of Odes* says:

> Yin's mirror is not remote,
> It lay with the age of the Xia. [#255]" (4A.2)

[Mencius here warns rulers of the day to take heed of the reigns of the ignominious rulers of the ninth century BCE, Kings Yu and Li—just as

---

15   Mo Di is commonly referred to as Mozi, Master Mo.

ode #255, the last couplet of which is cited by Mencius, warned the last ruler of the Shang, the tyrant Zhou, to heed the lessons to be learned from the reign of Jie, the cruel last ruler of the legendary Xia dynasty. Zhou failed to heed the warnings. Let not the present rulers be equally deaf to the infamy Yu and Li brought upon themselves and their families for generations to come.

The entire passage is an echo of the concept of the mandate of heaven (*tianming* 天命), introduced according to tradition in the early Zhou period, which holds that the right to rule is given, by heaven, to a person of most profound virtue, a person who puts the welfare of the people ahead of everything else. The right or mandate to rule is lost when the ruler shirks the responsibilities a true ruler has to the people and behaves instead in his own self-interest.]

13. Mencius said, "By being truly good the Three Dynasties won the empire; by not being good they lost the empire. A state too rises and falls, persists and perishes, by the same means. If the Son of Heaven is not truly good, he cannot preserve all within the four seas; if the feudal lord is not truly good, he cannot preserve the spirits of the soil and the grain [that protect his state]; if the high official is not truly good, he cannot preserve his ancestral temple; if the common person is not truly good, he cannot preserve his four limbs. Now, to despise death and yet delight in not being good is like despising drunkenness and yet indulging in strong wine. (4A.3)

[This passage continues the theme of the previous one. Under good kings, the Xia, Shang, and Zhou dynasties prospered; under bad kings, these three once-great dynasties met with their ruin. So, too, a person who does not cultivate goodness is sure to meet with his ruin.]

14. Mencius said, "There is a common saying among the people: 'The empire, the state, and the family': the foundation of the empire lies with the state; the foundation of the state lies with the family; the foundation of the family lies with the person." (4A.5)

[The saying, "The empire, the state, and the family," may circulate widely, but the relationship among the three bodies is not necessarily

well understood, according to Zhu Xi. Mencius thus elaborates
briefly, stating that the family is the foundation on which the state
is built, and, in turn, that the state is the foundation on which the
empire is built. Mencius, however, takes the popular saying one
significant step further, asserting that the family, in turn, has its beginnings in the cultivation of the individual. Everything thus rests with the
individual. Zhu comments here that this is why the *Great Learning* (#6)
states: "From the Son of Heaven on down to commoners, all without
exception should regard self-cultivation as the root." In citing this
passage from the *Great Learning*, Zhu ties the text of the *Great Learning* to
the text of the *Mencius*, again demonstrating for his readers that there
is coherence among the canonical Four Books, that they do indeed
share a message.]

15.   Chunyu Kuan said, "Isn't it a matter of ritual that men and
women, in giving to and receiving from each other, are not to
touch?" Mencius said, "Yes, it is." He said, "Suppose a sister-in-law
is drowning: do you extend a hand to rescue her?" Mencius said, "If
a sister-in-law is drowning and you do not rescue her—this is to be
a cruel beast. Men and women, in giving to and receiving from each
other, are not to touch. Such is the ritual. But to extend a hand to
rescue a drowning sister-in-law is to weigh the circumstances and
act accordingly." He said, "Today, the empire is drowning but you,
sir, do not rescue it. Why is that?" Mencius said, "When the empire
is drowning, you rescue it with the Way. You want to rescue the
empire with a hand?" (4A.17)

[Mencius and Chunyu Kuan would seem to agree that circumstances
being what they are, one has little choice but to extend one's hand to
rescue a drowning woman—even in the face of a proscription against
men and women touching. Chunyu Kuan presses on, arguing analo-
gously that Mencius therefore has little choice but to extend his hand
to rescue a drowning empire. But Mencius returns to the exigency
argument, explaining that particular circumstances require particular
responses: in the case of a drowning woman, rescuing with a hand is
called for; in the case of a drowning empire, there is a more appropriate
response—governing with the Way.]

16. Mencius said, "There are three ways to be unfilial. To have no heir is the most serious. Shun married without informing his parents, because he feared that he would have no heir.[16] The view of the superior man is that this is the same as having informed his parents." (4A.26)

[The other two ways of being unfilial, according to the commentary, are to let parents, out of a desire to curry favor with them, lapse into unrighteousness, and to refuse to take up office even when one's family is poor and the parents aged. This passage, Zhu Xi remarks, speaks, as does the previous one (#15), to the importance of exigencies, of taking into account the particular circumstances of the moment and acting as just as one should under those circumstances. The normal ritual before marriage is to inform one's parents of one's intentions. But, Shun, knowing that his parents would not have consented (cf. *Mencius* 5A.2), did not inform them, fearing that in the end he would leave no heirs behind. The superior man appreciates that although Shun did not practice the prescribed ritual, he nonetheless did precisely the right thing under the circumstances. Exigency on occasion trumps ritual.]

17. Mencius said, "The actualization of true goodness is serving our parents; the actualization of righteousness is obeying our elder brothers; the actualization of wisdom is understanding these two [true goodness and righteousness] and never departing from them; the actualization of rites is the regulation and adornment of these two. The actualization of music is taking delight in these two. Where there is delight they come to life, and once they come to life how can they be stopped? And when they cannot be stopped, our feet and hands will begin to dance without our realizing it. (4A.27)

[True goodness, righteousness, propriety, wisdom, and musical harmony inhere in every individual's human nature. But, they must be put into practice. Zhu observes that serving our parents and obeying our elder

---

16 For the story of Shun's marriage, see the *Mencius* 5A.2.

brothers, spoken of here, are simply expressions of our innate good mind, which Mencius speaks of in #32. Zhu further comments that this passage is what Confucius meant in #2 of the *Analects:* "filial piety and fraternal respect: are they not the root of practicing true goodness?" This is another instance of Zhu reading and understanding the Four Books intertextually, persuaded that the four do indeed constitute a coherent whole. Note that propriety, wisdom, and musical harmony are put in the service of true goodness and righteousness—the foundational virtues.]

18.   Mencius said, "When the sovereign is truly good, everybody will be truly good; when the sovereign is righteous, everybody will be righteous." (4B.5)

[The truly good ruler exerts a kind of moral charisma or moral force over his people. That is, his moral example possesses a power to draw the people to the good.]

19.   Mencius said, "Ritual that is not ritual, righteousness that is not righteousness—these are things the great person does not practice." (4B.6)

[Zhu comments here that ritual that is not ritual and righteousness that is not righteousness result from an inadequate investigation of principle. The great person, the person who understands principle thoroughly, will in all circumstances accord with it and thus always behave just as he should.

Mencius seems, too, to be suggesting in this brief comment that sincerity is crucial, that it is the authenticity of feeling that makes the practice of ritual and of righteousness truly efficacious.]

20.   Mencius said, "Only a person who refuses to act in some matters is capable of action in others." (4B.8)

[Master Cheng comments that a person who refuses to act is making a deliberate choice. Capable of refusing to act in some matters, such a person is capable of deciding to take deliberate action in others. The suggestion here is that knowing when it is appropriate to act and when it is appropriate not to act requires sound moral judgment.]

21. Mencius said, "The great person is one who does not lose his mind-and-heart of a child." (4B.11)

[The great person is great precisely because he has not been led astray by things. Not having been led astray, he holds on to his original mind-and-heart, which is thoroughly pure and without falsity. The great person then is one who does not let selfish or creaturely desires triumph over the goodness endowed in him at birth.]

22. Mencius said, "The superior man advances persistently along the proper path, hoping to get it for himself. Getting it for himself he rests in it at ease; resting in it at ease he trusts in it deeply; trusting in it deeply he penetrates its source in whatever is around him. It is for this reason that the superior man hopes to get it for himself." (4B.14)

[The student must be diligent in his studies, working tirelessly to arrive at an understanding that he can claim as his own. The understanding he seeks is the understanding of principle. Having acquired a true understanding of principle, he will confidently rely on it in all that he does.]

23. Mencius said, "Slight is the difference between man and beast. The common person lets go of it; the superior man holds on to it. Shun was insightful about the world around him and observant of human relationships. The source of his actions was true goodness and righteousness; it was not just that he was practicing acts of true goodness and righteousness." (4B.19)

[Mencius never explains wherein the small difference lies. Zhu Xi's commentary, for better or worse, does. All things, man and beast alike, he says, are endowed by heaven with principle as their nature. In that sense man and beast are similar. But they also are endowed by heaven with *qi*. It is here where the difference is to be found, for the *qi* that man receives is much more refined and balanced than that received by beasts. And, because his *qi* is that much more refined and balanced, he has the capability of maintaining whole his nature and thereby giving realization to principle—whereas beasts have no such capability. The superior man, conscious of this "small difference," cultivates it; the common person, not conscious of it, lets go of it, and, consequently, becomes no different from beasts. The meeting of classical Confucianism and Song metaphysics could hardly be more vivid than it is here. The last line of this passage has been read variously; I follow Zhu's reading.]

24.   Mencius said, "Where the superior man differs from others is in retaining his mind-and-heart. The superior man retains in his mind-and-heart both true goodness and a sense of propriety. To be truly good is to love others; to have a sense of propriety is to show respect for others. Those who love others will always be loved by others; those who respect others will always be respected by others. Suppose there is a person who treats me badly. The superior man is sure to look within himself: 'It must be that I am not truly good; it must be that I have no sense of propriety. Why, otherwise, should this have happened?' He looks within himself but finds that he is truly good; he looks within himself but finds that he has a sense of propriety. And yet, the bad treatment continues. The superior man is sure to look within himself: 'It must be that I don't do my utmost.' He looks within himself but finds that he does do his utmost. And yet, the bad treatment continues. The superior man says, 'This is one reckless person. If it be so, what is there to choose between him and a beast? And, is there any point in rebuking a beast?

"Thus the superior man has perpetual anxiety, but he has no unexpected troubles. Here is what he is anxious about: 'Shun was a man, and so too am I. Shun served as a model for the empire, a model that could be passed on to later generations. But I am nothing more than a common villager.' This is something one can be anxious about. How is one to deal with the anxiety? Simply be like Shun, and that is all. As for unexpected troubles, the superior man has none. What is not truly good he does not do; what does not accord with ritual he does not practice. Although unexpected troubles may arise, the superior man is not troubled by them." (4B.28)

[What is required to be a superior man is nothing more than holding on to the original mind-and-heart (see #21), for it is here that true goodness and propriety are found. If one can extend true goodness and propriety toward others, one is sure to be treated with goodness and propriety by others in return. Thus, the superior man is anxious lest he let go of the original mind-and-heart. What made Shun a model for the empire was that he had not let go. The lesson here is twofold: a mere villager, if vigilant about not letting go, can become a Shun; and, unexpected troubles will not trouble a person who is of fixed mind-and-heart, that is, who has not let go of the original mind-and-heart.]

25.   Wang Zhang said, "Did Yao give the empire to Shun?" Mencius said, "No. The Son of Heaven cannot give the empire to another." "If this is the case, and Shun got possession of the empire, who gave it to him?" "Heaven gave it to him." "In giving it to him did heaven present the mandate in great detail?" Mencius said, "No. Heaven did not speak but simply made it [the mandate] known through Shun's personal conduct and conduct of affairs." He said, "How did it go about making it known through his personal conduct and conduct of affairs?" He said, "The Son of Heaven can recommend a person to heaven but cannot compel heaven to give him the empire. Feudal lords can recommend others to the Son of Heaven but cannot compel the Son of Heaven to give them feudal lordships. Great officials can recommend others to feudal lords but cannot compel feudal lords to give them great office. In olden times, Yao recommended Shun to heaven, and heaven accepted him; he introduced him to the people and the people accepted him. Thus it is said, 'Heaven did not speak but simply made it known through his personal conduct and his conduct of affairs.' " He said, "Yao recommended him to heaven, and heaven accepted him; he introduced him to the people, and the people accepted him. I venture to ask, how did all this come about?" He said, "He had him preside over the sacrificial offerings and the hundred spirits accepted them. This was heaven accepting him. He had him preside over the affairs of the

empire and the affairs were well ordered. The people were content with him. This was the people accepting him. Heaven gave it to him and the people gave it to him. Therefore it is said, 'The Son of Heaven cannot give the empire to another.'

"Shun assisted Yao for twenty-eight years. People aren't capable of bringing this about. Heaven is. Yao died and when the three years of mourning were over, Shun left Yao's son for south of the South River. When feudal lords of the empire had imperial audiences, they did not go to Yao's son but to Shun; those with legal disputes to settle did not go to Yao's son but to Shun. Those singing praises sang the praises not of Yao's son but of Shun. It is on account of all this that I say, 'Heaven.' Only afterward did he return to the Middle Kingdom and ascend the imperial throne there. If he had moved into Yao's palace and forced Yao's son out—this would have been usurpation. This wouldn't have been heaven giving it to him.

"This is what is meant when the 'Taishi' chapter [of the *Book of History*] says, 'Heaven sees what the people see; heaven hears what the people hear.' " (5A.5)

[Mencius goes to some lengths here to argue that succession is not determined by the Son of Heaven but by heaven itself. That heaven has chosen a successor is not signified through some detailed proclamation, but through the ideal behavior of the individual and the embrace of him by the people of the realm. This is why Mencius says, "Heaven gave it to him and the people gave it him." Whereas heaven is surely powerful, then, its mandate is shown by the people's acceptance of the ruler. This is the meaning of the well-known quotation from the *Book of History*.]

26.   A virtuous gentleman in the village makes friends with other virtuous gentlemen in the village. A virtuous gentleman in the state makes friends with other virtuous gentlemen in the state. A virtuous gentleman in the empire makes friends with other virtuous gentlemen in the empire. When friendship with other virtuous gentlemen in the empire is no longer enough, he proceeds to a consideration of the ancients. Reciting their poetry and studying their works— can he possibly not understand the sort of men they were? For this

reason, he takes into consideration the age in which they lived as well. This is to become friends with the ancients. (5B.8)

[The virtue of the virtuous gentleman radiates throughout the village, state, and empire, attracting other persons of virtue. This is a sentiment that echoes the Confucian ideal of a person's virtue having a strong attraction for others.

What is interesting here is the belief that a sincere person, through exhaustive study of the ancients—their poetry, their books (i.e., the classics), their era—can come to know, even make friends with, the ancients. Neo-Confucians, especially Zhu Xi, would pick up on the idea that through the study of the inspired words of the sages of the past, one could converse with them and thereby arrive at a deeper understanding of Confucian truths.]

27.   King Xuan of Qi asked about great ministers. Mencius said, "Your Majesty, which kind of great ministers are you inquiring about?" The king replied, "Aren't they all the same?" "No," Mencius said. "There are the ministers related to you. And there are the ministers of the various other surnames." The king said, "Please tell me about related ministers." Mencius said, "If the ruler is making grave mistakes they admonish him, but if they do so over and over and he takes no heed, they replace him." The color rushed from the king's face. Mencius said, "Your Majesty mustn't be taken aback. You asked me, and I dare not be anything less than candid." Only when the color returned to the king's face did he ask about the ministers from other families. Mencius said, "If the ruler is making mistakes, they admonish him, but if they do so over and over and he takes no heed, they leave him." (5B.9)

[King Xuan is surprised to discover that his own kinsmen would remove him from the throne. The very possibility that he could be deposed no doubt takes him aback, and the further possibility that the removal from the throne would come at the hands of those closest to him leaves him reeling. The commentary explains that there is in fact nothing surprising here. Kinsmen have a particular investment in holding on to the kingdom, in the continuation of the imperial line. Any grave mistake

by King Xuan could put the kingdom—and the family's control of
it—at risk. For this reason, kinsmen would, in the words of the commentary, "replace the sovereign and put on the throne a relative who
is worthy of it."]

28.   Gaozi said, "Human nature may be likened to the willow and
righteousness to cups and bowls. Making true goodness and righteousness out of human nature is like making cups and bowls out
of the willow." Mencius responded, "Are you able to make cups and
bowls by following the nature of the willow? It is only by doing
violence to the willow that you can make cups and bowls. If you
do violence to the willow in making cups and bowls, must you also
do violence to a person in making true goodness and righteousness?
It is sure to be words like yours that induce people everywhere to
regard goodness and righteousness as injurious." (6A.1)

[This is the beginning of Book 6, Part A, the portion of the text where
Mencius mounts the strongest and most sustained defense of his proposition that human beings are instinctively good. Gaozi figures prominently in this portion, taking a contrary position that human nature is
neither good nor evil.

   It is this book of the *Mencius* that perhaps best accounts for the great
esteem in which Neo-Confucians, and the tradition generally, held the
Mencius from the Song dynasty until the fall of imperial China. The
book, as we will see, is dedicated to a variety of questions relating to
human nature: What constitutes it? Why is it not always manifest? How
is it that it can become manifest? As these sorts of questions were central
to the concerns of thinkers like Zhu Xi, the special attraction of such
scholars to this book is unsurprising.

   Zhu's commentary on this passage warns that if people were to take
Gaozi's words seriously they would consider goodness and righteousness
as harmful to their persons and consequently never practice them.]

29.   Gaozi said, "Human nature is like swirling water. Cut a passage
for it in the east and it flows east; cut a passage for it in the west and
it flows west. There is no distinction in human nature between good
and bad just as there is no distinction in water between east and

west." Mencius said, "It is true that in the case of water there is no distinction between east and west. But is there no distinction between up and down? The goodness of human nature is like water's flowing downhill. Every person is good; all water flows downhill. Now, take water: hit it with your hand or jump into it and you can make it splash higher than your forehead; dam it up, then channel it, and you can make it climb a mountain. Can this possibly be the nature of water? It is circumstances [external to it] that make it so. That a person can be made to do what is not good is a matter of his nature being like that of water in this regard." (6A.2)

[As suggested by earlier passages, argument by analogy to nature is a strong characteristic of Mencius' writings. Water does not naturally flow east or west, Gaozi begins. Mencius, quick to pick up Gaozi's analogy, agrees with him, but takes Gaozi's position one crucial step further, observing that water, after all, does naturally flow downhill.

If a passage like this, arguing that human nature is naturally inclined in the direction of the good, is successful in persuading readers, it is not because of the power of logic behind the argument; it has more to do with the reader's willingness to extend his personal familiarity with the properties of water to the properties of something less familiar, in this case, human nature.]

30. Gaozi said, "Our constitution at birth is what is meant by nature." Mencius said, "Is to say, 'Our constitution at birth is what is meant by nature,' the same as saying, 'White is what is meant by white?' " "Yes," said Gaozi. "Is the white of a white feather the same as the white of white snow? And is the white of white snow the same as the white of a white gem?" "Yes." "That being the case, is the nature of a dog the same as the nature of an ox? And is the nature of an ox the same as human nature?" (6A.3)

[Zhu glosses the character *sheng* 生, which I translate as "constitution at birth," as "referring to the wherewithal of people and creatures to perceive and to move." Gaozi's point here is that all things *sheng*, alive with perception and movement, have the same nature. Mencius finds this proposition ludicrous, suggesting that whereas dogs, oxen, and

human beings all do indeed perceive and move, it can hardly be claimed
that they all have the same nature. Zhu concludes that Gaozi, hearing
what Mencius had to say, appreciated that he had been wrong and thus
did not respond.

Zhu Xi offers a lengthy commentary on #30 that glosses the passage
drawing on the *li/qi* metaphysics of the day. Part of it reads:

> The term "nature" refers to the principle [*li*] human beings
> receive from heaven; the term *sheng*, "constitution at birth,"
> refers to *qi*, the psychophysical stuff human beings receive from
> heaven. The nature is what is above form; the psychophysical
> stuff is what is within form. All human beings and creatures,
> at birth, are possessed of this nature, and all are possessed of
> this psychophysical stuff as well. From the point of view of
> psychophysical stuff, it would seem that human beings and
> other creatures, in their perceiving and moving, are no differ-
> ent. But from the point of view of principle, can other creatures
> possibly receive the complete endowment of true goodness,
> righteousness, propriety, and wisdom? This is why human
> nature is always good and is the guiding spirit of the ten thou-
> sand things. Gaozi does not understand human nature is prin-
> ciple but takes it as corresponding to psychophysical stuff.

Why Neo-Confucians found Book 6 of the *Mencius* so meaningful should
be apparent. So too should the process by which thinkers like Zhu Xi
reconciled the Four Books with a contemporary Song worldview. That
these ancient texts and the newly developed *li/qi* metaphysics are made,
in commentarial passages such as this, to shed light on each other
confers legitimacy on both. That is, the canonical texts, by addressing
the concerns that matter most to thinkers of the day, are shown to have
continued relevance in the Song; at the same time the metaphysical
understanding that could be found in these texts demonstrates that the
emerging metaphysics of the time is entirely consistent with classical
Confucian teachings.]

31.   Gaozi said, "Enjoying food and sex is our nature. True goodness is internal, not external. Righteousness is external, not internal." Mencius said, "Why do you say that goodness is internal and

righteousness external?" Gaozi replied, "It is because he is an elder that I treat him as an elder. It isn't that the 'elder' is to be found in me. This is the same as treating something as white because it is white. I am responding to the whiteness, which is external to me. Therefore I say it is external." Mencius said, "There may be no difference between treating as white the whiteness of a white horse and the whiteness of a white person, but is it true that there is no difference between the treatment of an elderly horse and of an elderly person? Consider further: Is it being elderly that is righteous? Or is it the treatment of the elderly that is righteous?"

Gaozi said, "Because he is my own younger brother I love him. Because he is the younger brother of a man from Qin I do not love him. Thus the feeling of love derives from myself; therefore I say it is internal. I regard the elderly from Chu with the respect due an elder; similarly I regard my own elderly with the respect due an elder. Thus the feeling of respect derives from elderliness; therefore I say it is external." Mencius said, "Relishing grilled meat from Qin is no different from relishing our own grilled meat. This is also the case with other things. Does this mean then that relishing grilled meat is external as well?" (6A.4)

[This debate is over the source of righteousness. Mencius, as we have seen earlier, especially in #8, believes it to be internal, part of human nature, together with goodness, propriety, and wisdom. Gaozi, although agreeing that goodness, which he associates with love for others, comes from within and is internal, argues that righteousness is external. We treat all elders, whether our own or those from Chu, in the same respectful manner simply because they are older. It is their characteristic of being older that gives rise to our treating them with the respect due elders. Mencius counters, suggesting that Gaozi's various positions are contradictory. Gaozi at the outset, after all, had proclaimed that the enjoyment of food is human nature. But if Gaozi is going to take the position that an indiscriminate respect for all elders demonstrates that righteous treatment of them has its source, externally, in their age, then our enjoyment of grilled meat, whether cooked by us or by the people of Qin, points to one of two possibilities. Either of these possibilities points up the inconsistency of Gaozi's general argument: (1) that our enjoyment of delicious grilled food, no matter who prepares it, does not necessarily derive internally, from human nature; or (2) that our respectful treatment of our elders, no matter where they are from, does not necessarily derive externally. The second possibility here would require Gaozi to concede that our righteous behavior toward others, like the enjoyment of food, has its source internally and is a matter of human nature.]

32.   Gongduzi said, "Gaozi says, 'In human nature there is neither good nor bad.' Others say, 'Human nature can be made to be good or made to be bad, which is why in the time of Wen and Wu the people were fond of goodness and in the time of Yu and Li[17] people were fond of malice.' Still others say, 'There is human nature that is good and human nature that is not good, which is why when Shun was ruler there still was Xiang,[18] why with Gusou[19] as his father there still was Shun, and why with Zhou[20] as son of their older brother and their ruler to boot there still were Viscount Qi of Wei and Prince Bigan.'[21] Now you say, 'Human nature is good.' Does this mean that these others are wrong?"

Mencius responded, "Our natural tendency is to do good. This is what I mean by its [i.e., the nature's] being good. Doing what is not good is not the fault of our natural disposition. Each and every one of us possesses the mind-and-heart of compassion; the mind-and-heart that is ashamed of evil in oneself and detests it in others; the mind-and-heart of respectfulness and reverence; and the mind-and-heart of right and wrong. The mind-and-heart of compassion is true goodness; the mind-and-heart that is ashamed of evil in oneself and hates it in others is righteousness; the mind-and-heart

---

17   Evil rulers during the early centuries of the Zhou; see #12.
18   The evil brother of the legendary and sage emperor Shun.
19   The evil father of Shun.
20   The evil last ruler of the Shang; see #6.
21   Zhu questions whether Qi, the viscount of Wei, was in fact the uncle of King Zhou. Both of these men, Viscount Qi and Prince Bigan, were held by the tradition to have remonstrated courageously and righteously with the evil Zhou, but to no good end.

of respectfulness and reverence is propriety; and the mind-and-heart of right and wrong is wisdom. True goodness, righteousness, propriety, and wisdom are not welded on to us from without. We possess them from the very beginning, but we just do not think about it. Thus it is said, 'Seek and you will find it; let go of it and you will lose it.' That some are at twice, five times, or an infinite remove from others in this respect is owing to their inability to give full realization to their natural disposition.

"The *Book of Odes* says,

Heaven gives birth to the multitude of people
Once there is a thing there is a norm for it.
Holding fast to what makes us human
People take delight in this excellent virtue of theirs. [#260]

Confucius said, 'Whoever wrote this ode knew the Way. Thus, once there is a thing, there is sure to be a norm for it. And because people hold fast to what makes us human, they take delight in this outstanding virtue of theirs.'" (6A.6)

[Because our nature is good our natural tendency is to do good. After all, each of us possesses the mind-and-heart that embraces the four cardinal virtues: true goodness, righteousness, propriety, and wisdom. Human nature, Master Cheng reminds the reader here, is one with principle. All of us have it; Yao and Shun have it and so too does the ordinary person. What separates the sage and the ordinary person is in the refinement of their *qi*. If everyone were to choose to engage in learning, to work to perfect the quality of their psychophysical endowment, and thereby to give expression to the goodness of their original nature, there would be no distinction among people in their moral behavior. That is, through learning, all people would realize the potential to follow the natural tendency toward goodness. People must not let go of what is originally theirs.

Noting that in #8 Mencius relates the mind-and-heart to the "seeds" of the four virtues and that here he relates it directly to the four virtues without any mention of seeds, Zhu remarks that the earlier passage was an expression of hope for the development of the virtues, whereas this one is referring to the practice of the virtues, now fully realized. This is an attempt—not necessarily persuasive—to reconcile an apparent inconsistency in the writings of Mencius, to show readers that the message of this central text is indeed internally coherent.] (6A.8)

33.   Mencius said, "The trees on Mt. Niu were once quite luxuriant. But as they were just on the outskirts of the capital, axes chopped them down one by one. Could they remain luxuriant? And yet, given the renewal that goes on day and night and the nourishment that rain and dew bring, shoots and buds never fail to sprout. But, then, cattle and sheep come to graze. This is what accounts for the bald appearance of the mountain. When people see its baldness, they assume it was never wooded. But could this really be the nature of the mountain?

The same is true of what belongs to a person: can he really be without the mind-and-heart of goodness and righteousness? His letting go of his originally good mind-and-heart is like the ax chopping down the trees: if day after day it is chopped away can it remain luxuriant? And yet, given the renewal that goes on day and night and the restorative vital energy that accompanies the dawn, his likes and dislikes will still bear some small resemblance to those of other people. But what he does during the day will fetter and destroy it [the originally good mind-and-heart] completely. If it is fettered repeatedly, the restorative vital energy of the nighttime will be insufficient to sustain it. And if the restorative vital energy of the nighttime is insufficient to sustain it, he will become little different from a beast. When others see a beast, they will assume that it never had a natural disposition for goodness. But could this really be the natural tendency of the man? Thus, if it receives nourishment there is nothing that will not grow; if it does not receive nourishment there is nothing that will not decay. Confucius said, 'Hold on to it and you preserve it; let go of it and you lose it. It comes and goes at no appointed times, and no one knows where it will settle.' Isn't it of the mind-and-heart that he speaks?"

[Mt. Niu, according to the commentary, is located in the southeast of the state of Qi, Mencius' native state. Zhu explains that the life force generated day and night by the ever-circulating *yin/yang* 陰陽 vital energy of the universe is restorative, bringing about renewal to both vegetation and the originally good mind-and-heart.

Although human beings are born with a natural goodness, that goodness is easily obscured by the effects of external circumstances and things. Because it is easily obscured, the manifestation of its potential is uncertain, indeed quite precarious. To realize goodness in practice, therefore, requires our determined effort to hold on to the original mind-and-heart of goodness and righteousness. "It comes and goes at no appointed times" is a warning that whether we achieve the goodness—or not—is entirely in our own hands. If we do not work at cultivating our natural goodness, it will be no more apparent than is the natural luxuriance of Mt. Niu.]

34.   Mencius said, "Fish are what I desire; so too are bear claws. If I cannot have both of them I'll give up the fish and choose the bear claws. Life is what I desire; so too is righteousness. If I cannot have both of them I'll give up life and choose righteousness. Life, to be sure, is what I desire, but there is that which I desire even more than life. Thus, I will not choose life at its expense. Death, to be sure, is what I loathe, but there is that which I loathe even more than death. Therefore, there will be calamities that I cannot avoid. Supposing a person desires nothing more than life: he will employ whatever means necessary to stay alive. Supposing a person loathes nothing more than death: there is nothing whatsoever he will not do to avoid calamity. When a person follows his originally good mind-and-heart, there are means he will not employ even to remain alive; when a person follows this mind-and-heart, there are things he will not do even if they enable him to avoid calamity. Therefore, we have that which we desire more than life and that which we loathe more than death. It is not the worthy person alone who possesses such a mind-and-heart; all people possess it. But the worthy person never loses it, that's all.

A basketful of rice, a bowlful of soup: getting them means staying alive and not getting them means dying. If they are offered in an insulting manner, a commoner walking along the road would not accept them; if they are offered only after being trampled on, a

beggar would not condescend to take them. But if there is an emolument of ten thousand bushels of grain, we accept it without considering propriety and righteousness. Of what benefit is ten thousand
bushels to us? Is it for the beautification of our homes; for the
support of our wives and concubines; for the sake of winning the
gratitude of our poverty-stricken acquaintances? What earlier we
would not accept even if it meant our death we now accept for the
beautification of our homes. What earlier we would not accept even
if it meant our death we now accept for the support of our wives
and concubines. What earlier we would not accept even if it meant
our death we now accept in order to win the gratitude of acquaintances who are poverty-stricken. Can we not put a stop to this? This
is what is called 'losing one's original mind-and-heart.' " (6A.10)

[Zhu concedes that desiring life and despising death are normal feelings; but, more natural still, because of our original mind-and-heart, is
a concern for righteousness. Life and death matter more than righteousness only when an individual has abandoned the mind-and-heart,
innate in all of us, that is ashamed of evil in oneself and hates it in
others.]

35.   Mencius said, "True goodness (*ren* 仁) is the mind-and-heart
of a person (*ren* 人); righteousness is his path. How pitiable it is to
give up the path and follow it no longer; to let go of the mind and
not know enough to seek after it. A person who has lost chickens
and dogs knows to seek after them; yet when he loses the mind-and-
heart he does not know enough to seek after it. The way of learning
is nothing more than to seek after this lost mind-and-heart."
(6A.11)

[True goodness and righteousness may be innate but practicing them
requires effort. Excessive feelings and selfish desires too easily sidetrack
us, becoming obstacles to the manifestation of the virtues that are our
natural endowment. Learning, Zhu remarks, is about making our allotment of *qi* clear and bright, about bringing a balance to it, so that
emotions and desires do nothing to prevent the external expression of
the goodness within.]

36.   Gongduzi asked, "If we are all equally human, why do some become great persons and others become small persons?" Mencius said, "Those who accord with the body in its great aspects become great persons; those who accord with the body in its small aspects become small persons." Gongduzi said, "If we are all equally human, why do some accord with the body in its great aspects and some accord with the body in its small aspects?" Mencius responded, "Since the function of the eyes and ears does not include the ability to think, they are misled by other creaturely things. When a thing mingles with other things, it can easily be led astray. The function of the mind-and-heart is to think; if it does its thinking it will get it, but if it doesn't it will not. This is what heaven gives to us. If we first take our stand on what is great [i.e., the mind-and-heart], then what is small is unable to do violence to it. It is this and this alone that makes for the great person." (6A.15)

[This passage picks up the theme of the previous passage, #35. We all have what is great within, but some of us develop it, whereas others do not. It comes down to a matter of choice; we need to fix our will, or, in the words of Mencius here, "first take our stand on what is great." Here, as in other passages of the *Mencius,* we are returned to the importance given the will by Confucius earlier. If the will is not set on developing the great, the person is prone to be misled by creaturely things; misled by creaturely things, he becomes subject to selfish desires, which, in turn, obstruct his inner goodness from shining forth.]

37.   Mencius said, "In teaching others to shoot with bow and arrow, Archer Yi was always determined to draw the bow to the full. Students too were always determined to draw the bow to the full. In teaching others carpenters always use the compass and square. Students too always use the compass and square." (6A.20)

[Likewise, in teaching disciples the principles of morality, a master must be determined to rely on the necessary tools, namely, the Way of the sages.]

38. Jiao of Cao asked, "Isn't it true that 'all people can become a Yao or Shun'?" Mencius said, "Yes, it is." "I, Jiao, have heard that King Wen was ten Chinese feet (*chi*) and that Tang was nine feet. Today, I am nine feet four inches (*cun*) tall. But besides eating I have no capabilities. What can I do to become a Yao or Shun?" "What does that have to do with height? Just behave like them and nothing more. Suppose there is a person whose strength is not up to lifting even a duck. He would be a weak person. But today he says, 'I can lift three thousand pounds and am a strong person.' If this be the case and he can lift as heavy a load as Wu Huo, then he has indeed become a Wu Huo, and that's all there is to it. People are distressed by their inability to do it. The problem, however, is simply that they don't do it.

"To walk slowly behind one's elders is what is called behavior befitting a younger brother; to walk quickly ahead of one's elders is what is called behavior not befitting a younger brother. As for those who walk quickly ahead, is it that they are incapable? It's that they don't do it! The way of Yao and Shun is nothing but filial and brotherly respect. Wear the clothes of Yao, recite the words of Yao, behave as Yao behaved: this is all it takes to be a Yao. Wear the clothes of Jie, recite the words of Jie, behave as Jie behaved: this is all it takes to be a Jie."

"If I can get a meeting with the ruler of Zou and arrange for the use of lodgings, I would like to stay here and receive instruction from you." "The Way is like a great road. It is not difficult to come to know. People are at fault: they simply do not seek it. Go home and seek it there; you'll have more than enough teachers." (6B.2)

[Anybody can become a Yao or Shun since everybody is endowed with precisely the same human nature. It is merely a matter of fixing our will on behaving as we should. It is for this reason that Jiao need not take Mencius as his teacher. He has his own internal teacher; he must simply set his mind on following it. This accessibility to sagehood is a message that Neo-Confucians from the Song through the twentieth century found especially appealing.]

39. Mencius said, "A person, in giving full realization to his mind-and-heart, knows his nature; and knowing his nature, he knows heaven. By preserving his mind-and-heart and nurturing his nature, he serves heaven. Whether his life is to be short or long does not weigh on him; he cultivates himself and waits for death. This is how he stands firm in his fate." (7A.1)

[Zhu, in his quite lengthy commentary on this brief passage, draws heavily on the metaphysics of the day. The mind-and-heart, he says, contains the myriad manifestations of principle, enabling human beings to respond to the myriad affairs of the world as we should. Human nature is principle, likewise contained in the mind-and-heart. To probe thoroughly the mind-and-heart, to reach an understanding of the myriad manifestations of principle therein, is thus to come to an understanding of human nature. Another way of putting this is that the mind-and-heart is the locus of the seeds of true goodness, righteousness, propriety, and wisdom, the four cardinal virtues that constitute our human nature. To give full development or realization to those seeds is to give full realization to human nature. Zhu further reminds the reader that principle, which in human beings is identical with human nature, issues forth from heaven and thus to know human nature is to know the intentions of heaven; knowing heaven's intentions, we can behave in accord with them. What is fated for us—our longevity, our prosperity—we cannot control, but we do decide whether to cultivate ourselves, to give full realization to our mind-and-heart, or not.

Master Cheng is cited here: "The mind-and-heart, human nature, and heaven are all of one principle. When speaking of it as principle we call it heaven; when speaking of it as what is endowed in us we call it human nature; when speaking of it as what is preserved in people we call it the mind-and-heart."]

40. Mencius said, " 'Seek and you will find it, let it go and you will lose it.' This is a seeking that helps in the getting; it is the seeking inside oneself. 'Seeking is to follow a proper course; getting is a matter of fate.' This is a seeking that is of no help in the getting; it is the seeking outside oneself." (7A.3)

[Seeking what is internal—true goodness, righteousness, propriety, and wisdom—is worthwhile, for the "getting" is up to us. Seeking what is external—wealth and status—is not worthwhile, for the getting of it is a matter of fate, outside of our control. See #39.]

42. Mencius said, "The ten thousand things are all complete within me. Nothing brings greater joy than to look within and find that I am true to myself. Try your hardest to treat others empathetically—this is the shortest way to true goodness." (7A.4)

[In Zhu's reading, the ten thousand things are to be understood as the *principle that inheres in the ten thousand things*. This principle inheres in each human being as our human nature. It is in our embodiment of this principle, common to all things, that all things are complete within us. Logic thus has it, according to Zhu, that to be true to ourselves is to be true to this principle, and that to be true to principle, in turn, is to be true to the ten thousand things—which means treating them as they ought to be treated. Hence the profound joy. The person who has yet to reach this stage is advised by Mencius to bring his own true goodness to perfection through the mindful practice of empathy (*shu*) toward others. He is to treat others as he himself would wish to be treated. As Confucius had said earlier in the *Analects* (e.g., #19, #34, #94), the practice of empathy comes close to the practice of true goodness.]

43. Mencius said, "In doing it, he does not understand it clearly; in practicing it repeatedly, he does not examine it carefully. For his entire life he follows it but does not know it is the Way: this characterizes the multitude of people." (7A.5)

[In conversations with disciples Zhu explains that the problem here is that people generally do not understand, in the matter at hand, "principle as it ought to be"; nor do they examine why "the principle is as it is" in that same matter.[22] Again, this is not an issue of capability on their part but of choice. They do not set their minds on learning.]

---

22 YL 60.1439.

44. Mencius said, "A person must not be without shame. One who is ashamed though he has not done anything shameful will never get caught up in anything shameful."[23] (7A.6)

45. Mencius said, "What people are able to do without having learned it—this is innate, good ability. What they know without having pondered it—this is innate, good knowledge. There is no child of two or three years who does not know to love his parents; as they grow up, there is none who does not know to respect his elder brothers. To treat parents with the love due parents is a matter of true goodness; to treat elders with the respect due elders is a matter of righteousness—and nothing more. This is true everywhere under heaven." (7A.15)

[The commentary remarks, "Loving one's parents and respecting one's elders are matters of innate good ability and innate good knowledge." Both loving one's parents and respecting one's elders are innate in that they are matters of true goodness (*ren*) and righteousness (*yi*).]

46. Mencius said, "Do not do what should not be done; do not desire what should not be desired. This is all there is to it." (7A.17)

[Selfish thoughts cannot but arise; they must be checked, however. To check them, look within at the mind-and-heart that is ashamed of evil in oneself and hates it in others, and develop it to its fullest.]

47. Mencius said, "Yangzi was barely up to caring for himself.[24] If by plucking out just one hair he could benefit the whole world, he

---

23 In this terse statement of but thirteen characters there are four occurrences of *chi* 恥, which can be variously translated as "shame," "to feel or be ashamed," "shameful," and "a sense of shame." One can understand the saying in a number of ways, and indeed commentators have. This is Zhu's reading according to his commentary.

24 Zhu glosses the character *qu* 取 in the first line, normally understood as "to choose," as *jinzu* 僅足, "barely or almost adequate." It is a rather strange gloss, but he provides no explanation.

would not do it. Mozi loved universally. If by abrading his body from head to heel, he could benefit the whole world, he would do it. Zimo held fast to a middle course between the two; and by holding fast to a middle course he came close to it [the Way]. But holding fast to a middle course, if there be no weighing of circumstances, is the same as holding fast to a single fixed position. What I dislike about holding fast to a single fixed position is that it does harm to the Way. Taking a single fixed position disregards a hundred others." (7A.26)

[Mencius speaks of Yang Zhu and Mo Di in #11 as well. Zhu comments that Zimo was a worthy from the state of Lu; little else is known about him.

This is an interesting passage, especially read in conjunction with the last of the Four Books, *Maintaining Perfect Balance*. The point here is that following a "middle course" has no special merit per se. Mencius acknowledges that in the case of Zimo, following a middle course between Yangzi and Mozi did indeed bring him close to the Way. But Mencius warns the reader not to generalize from Zimo's case. To be *zhong* 中, he asserts, is not to hold unwaveringly to an abstract middle course; nor is it simply the pursuit of moderation in one's behavior. It is to weigh ever-changing circumstances and to judge what is appropriate—morally appropriate—in those circumstances. Moral sensitivity and flexibility are called for, not moral obstinacy. Zhu glosses the passage as follows: " 'Caring for oneself' does harm to true goodness; 'loving universally' does harm to righteousness; 'holding fast to a middle course' does harm to doing what is appropriate under the circumstances." To be truly *zhong*, then, means something like maintaining perfect moral balance in whatever the circumstances.

The problem with Mozi's "loving universally" is that it undermines the Confucian principle of graded love, where love for closer relations, such as a father or brother, is thought to be naturally stronger than love for a mere acquaintance or a stranger.]

48. Mencius said, "Our body and our appearance are part of our heavenly given nature. It is the sage alone who can give fulfillment to his body." (7A.38)

[In talking with students Zhu remarks that the appearance belongs to the body and comes into existence only once the body exists.[25] This explains why Mencius, in the second sentence, speaks only of giving fulfillment to the body; the appearance is implied.

Zhu comments: "Every person's body and appearance have principle, which we call human nature. *Jian* 踐, 'give fulfillment,' is the *jian* of *jianyan* 踐言, 'to fulfill a promise.' Now, although the multitude might have this body, they are unable to realize its principle. As a result, they cannot give fulfillment to their bodies. The sage has this body, but moreover is able to realize its principle; once he has done so he can give perfect fulfillment to his body—and be free of all regrets." For Cheng and Zhu, then, this remark by Mencius is about cultivating human nature—and all of its potentialities—to perfection.]

49.   Mencius said, "There are five ways the superior man teaches others: by transforming them, as seasonal rain transforms vegetation; by perfecting their virtue; by developing their talents; by answering their questions; and by training them indirectly through the transmission of his learning. These are the five ways he teaches others." (7A.40)

50.   Mencius said, "When the Way prevails under heaven, let the Way accompany your person wherever it goes; when the Way does not prevail, let your person accompany the Way wherever it goes. Never have I heard of the Way following behind a person." (7A.42)

[A person goes forth only if confident that the Way is being put into practice; when the Way is in retreat a person should feel obliged to follow it. The two should always be in each other's company. The person, and here of course is meant the potential official, must take into account the whereabouts and condition of the Way. The sentiment here is similar to the one expressed in #48 of the *Analects:* "When the Way prevails under heaven, show yourself; when the Way does not prevail,

---

25 YL 60.1451.

remain hidden." Of course, a different view is found in *Analects* #105 and #106, where the Master insists that a good Confucian is obliged never to give up, never to retreat in the face of a society that has lost the Way. It is precisely his duty to bring the Way to society.]

51.   Mencius said, "A person who stops where he ought not stop will stop anywhere. A person who slights one who ought to be treated generously will slight anyone. A person who is keen to advance will be quick to retreat." (7A.44)

52.   Mencius said, "The superior man loves creatures but does not treat them with true goodness [which is due people alone]; he treats people with true goodness but is not intimate with them [which is due only one's relatives]. Being intimate with relatives, he treats people with true goodness; treating people with true goodness, he loves creatures." (7A.45)

[Mencius here is attacking Mozi's idea that we should love all creatures and things equally, arguing instead that feelings of love are naturally strongest for those closest to us, namely, our family and, in particular, our parents. The commentary notes that the mind-and-heart of true goodness can be extended only to other human beings, not to creatures.

The commentary goes on to cite three Neo-Confucians of the Song, all of whom remark that the passage is illustrative of the Song belief that principle is one, but its manifestations are many. Love for, true goodness toward, and intimacy with relatives are, in fact, all matters of true goodness; they simply are different manifestations of it in different relationships.]

53.   Mencius said, "If a person does not practice the Way, it will not be practiced by his wife and children; if in giving orders to others he does not accord with the Way, he will be unable to get even his wife and children to comply." (7B.9)

[Moral accord begins with the head of the family. So too does moral example. A father who is upright teaches uprightness to his wife and children and, at the same time, produces familial order.]

54. Mencius said, "If there be no trust invested in the good and the worthy, the state will seem an empty shell; if there be no rites and righteousness, confusion between upper and lower will prevail; if there be no administration of government, state finances will be insufficient." (7B.12)

[For a state to prosper, socially and economically, the good and the worthy must be employed by the ruler.]

55. Mencius said, "The people are the most important; the spirits of earth and grain come next; and the ruler is the least important. Thus, win over the peasants to become the ruler; win over the Son of Heaven to become a feudal lord; win over the feudal lord to become a high official. When a feudal lord imperils the altar to the spirits of earth and grain, he is replaced. When the sacrificial animals are prepared, the offerings of grain purified, and the observance of the sacrifices timely, but there is still drought and flooding, the altars to the spirits of earth and grain are replaced." (7B.14)

[The highest position is won only when the people, in their mind-and-heart, are won. Having won their mind-and-heart, the ruler goes on to establish altars to the spirits of earth and grain, spirits whose responsibility it is to protect the people from natural disasters. The altars to these spirits thus signify the establishment of the state and the responsibility of the ruler to maintain the people's favor. Mencius notes that a feudal lord who does not tread the true path is sure to lose the favor of the spirits. In turn, they will no longer be responsive or efficacious. As a consequence, the people will replace their lord. Droughts and floods, in particular, are a signal that the spirits have abandoned the people and that the altars need to be replaced.]

56. Mencius said, "A sage is a teacher for a hundred generations. Such is the case with Bo Yi and Liuxia Hui. Thus, in hearing about Bo Yi the corrupt become pure and the weak grow determined; in hearing about Liuxia Hui the petty become generous and the narrow-minded become tolerant. These inspired the first one hundred generations and, in the second one hundred generations,

anyone who heard tell of them was moved to rejuvenation. If not
sages how could they have had this effect? Just imagine the effect
they had on those who received direct instruction from them."
(7B.15)

[Bo Yi, of the early Zhou, went into reclusion out of refusal to serve the
Zhou, believing that the Zhou had come to power by force and was not
a legitimate successor to the Shang. Liuxia Hui was an official in the
state of Lu who refused to give up hope of reforming society even in
the face of impure rulers.]

57.   Mencius said, "The worthies, in their luminosity, made others
luminous; nowadays people, themselves in darkness, try to make
others luminous." (7B.20)

[The commentary ties this remark by Mencius to the first line of the
Great Learning, saying that "the Way of great learning lies in letting one's
inborn luminous virtue shine forth"; this luminous virtue shines forth
on family, state, and empire, and—through the power of moral influence—brings about a similar effect in others.]

58.   Mencius said to the disciple Gaozi,[26] "Consider a narrow track
in the mountains: use it briefly and it becomes a path; abandon it
for a short while and weeds will cover it over. Right now your mind-
and-heart is covered over by weeds." (7B.21)

[The commentary explains: the mind-and-heart of principle and righteousness must not be obstructed in the least.]

59.   Mencius said, "Yao and Shun were ones who naturally [without
cultivation] manifested human nature; Tang and Wu, they returned
to it [through cultivation]. When every movement and every expression accords perfectly with ritual, this is virtue at its fullest. Being

---

26 Not to be confused with his rival philosopher who appears especially prominently in Book 6.

sorrowful in mourning the dead is not for the sake of impressing
the living. Being constant in pursuit of virtue, without deviation,
is not for the sake of winning emolument. Being unfailingly trust-
worthy in one's words is not for the sake of conforming to proper
behavior. The superior man follows the norm and awaits his fate,
and that is all. (7B.33)

["The norm" (*fa* 法) is glossed in the commentary as "heavenly principle as it ought to be" (天理之當然者). Mencius urges us in this passage
to do what is demanded by "principle as it ought to be," without other
considerations. That is, we are to do good for its own sake. As the commentary notes, good fortune and prosperity are fated by heaven and
unrelated to anything we do. We can control our own moral development, nothing more. Consider #39 and #40.

In a brief comment, Master Cheng notes that the phrase "to return
to the nature," an idea dear to Neo-Confucians, has its origins
here with Mencius. Comments such as this help explain why Neo-
Confucians in the Song came to place great value on this text and to
give it, together with the other three of the Four Books, precedence
over the Five Classics.]

60.   Mencius said, "There is no better way to nurture the mind-
and-heart than to have few desires. Here is a person with few
desires: there may be occasions when he fails to preserve it [the
original mind-and-heart], but they will be few. Here is a person with
many desires: there may be occasions when he preserves it, but they
will be few." (7B.35)

[This is a warning to students that if they wish to hold on to the original
mind-and-heart—and realize true goodness—they must work to keep
desires few.]

Maintaining Perfect Balance

MAINTAINING PERFECT BALANCE[27] 中庸

[Zhu Xi glosses the title as follows: "*Zhong* is a term meaning 'neither to one side nor the other; neither to overshoot nor to fall short.' *Yong* means 'normal or constant.'" Immediately after the title, Zhu adds the following introduction to the text, which the later tradition treats as part of the classic itself:]

The Masters Cheng said, "To lean neither to one side nor the other is what is called *zhong* ('maintaining perfect balance'); unchanging is what is called *yong* ('normal or constant'). Perfect balance is the true Way of the universe; the constant is the steadfast principle of the universe. This work presents the method of the mind-and-heart as passed down from generation to generation by the Confucian school. Fearing that over time mistakes would arise, Zisi wrote it down in the text we have here, passing it on to Mencius. In the beginning the text speaks of the one principle; in the middle, it unfolds to treat the myriad things; and in the end, it brings them together again as the one principle. Unfurl it and it fills every corner of the universe; roll it back up and it retreats [into the mind-and-heart], wrapping itself in secrecy. Its flavor is inexhaustible. The whole of it is practical learning. The skilled reader turns it over and over in his mind, and once he gets it, draws on it his whole life, finding that it has no limits."[28]

---

[27] *Maintaining Perfect Balance* is a text in thirty-three chapters, subdivided into paragraphs.

[28] Whereas some scholars as early as the Han had suggested a connection between Zisi and *Maintaining Perfect Balance*, it is only in the Song, with Zhu Xi, that the attribution of authorship to Zisi becomes generally accepted by the tradition. The case for attribution, however, is based on limited textual evidence and thus has been called into considerable question, especially beginning in the Qing period (1644–1912).

[*Zhong* 中, the first character in the title, means "maintaining perfect balance" and brings to mind passages in the *Analects* (e.g., 6.29, which is cited almost word for word below, in ch. 3.1) and the *Mencius* (passage #47). "To maintain perfect balance," according to Zhu's remarks here and in commentary to these passages in the *Analects* and the *Mencius*, is to weigh circumstances and find the perfect balance, behaving precisely as demanded by the particular circumstances. This requires that we exercise sensitive judgment, balancing the various considerations against one another. "Maintaining perfect balance" is never going too far or falling short, never leaning to one side or the other, and consequently is to behave just as we should in each and every situation in life. This is where the second character, *yong* 庸, comes in, according to Zhu. Glossing the character as "normal or constant," he understands *yong*, as had Master Cheng before him, to refer to steadfast principle (*dingli* 定理). Only by carefully considering each set of circumstances, and following the perfectly appropriate, perfectly balanced course of action called for by those circumstances, can one unfailingly accord with steadfast principle.

When disciples, in conversation with Zhu, note that his gloss of *yong*, "normal or constant," appearing just after the title, differs from Master Cheng's reference to it as "unchanging," he explains that the term "constant" carries the meaning of "unchanging." It is only because *yong* is constant that it is unchanging. He then adds that Cheng's gloss, "unchanging," refers to "unchanging principle." Elaborating, he says, "*yong* (normal or constant) most definitely refers to steadfast principle, but if we were to gloss it straightforwardly as steadfast principle, people wouldn't understand its sense of normal or constant. Now when we speak of 'normal or constant,' steadfast principle is naturally implied."[29]

Students, reflecting on Zhu's glosses of the two title words, repeatedly ask him how ongoing assessment of the different behavior required in life's different circumstances—which allows for, indeed requires, sensitive judgment and behavioral flexibility—can be reconciled with adhering to fixed principle. He explains that by weighing the circumstances

---

29 YL 62.1481–1484, inter alia.

at hand and acting as one should in those particular circumstances, one is certain, at all times, to be in accord with universal principle-as-it-ought-to-be.[30] Never does a person who so acts depart from the right Way. Therefore, one is in accord with principle or the Way when one adjusts one's conduct appropriately to changing circumstances.

Thus, a loose paraphrase of the title, *Zhongyong,* as Zhu Xi glosses it, would read something like "maintaining perfect balance in each and every set of circumstances and thus keeping to steadfast principle at all times."

For brevity's sake, I have adopted the translation "maintaining perfect balance," recognizing that it does not convey fully Zhu's complex understanding of the title nor the difficult relationship that he posits between the separate terms *zhong* and *yong. Maintaining Perfect Balance: Keeping to the Way Amidst Change* would, I think, better reflect Zhu's explanation but is much too cumbersome.

The conventional translation, the *Mean* or the *Doctrine of the Mean,* is problematic in any event. It fails Zhu's reading on at least two important counts: first—much like my own—it makes no attempt to deal with the second character in the title, *yong;* and, second, the word "mean," implying some vague "middle way" between two extremes, does little to express Zhu's sense of *zhong* as dedicated reflection, as a subtle and ongoing process of sustaining perfect moral balance in life's infinitely variable circumstances. *Zhong* is not, for Zhu, simply to pursue a middle course or to behave in moderation, as the term "mean" suggests.

Whereas historically there has been considerable debate over the authorship of the *Zhongyong,* the attribution here to Zisi in the opening remarks, however sound, has two far-reaching implications. One, with the assertion that Zengzi, Confucius' disciple, authored the *Great Learning* and that Zisi, Confucius' grandson, authored *Maintaining Perfect Balance,* Zhu gives to the Four Books a pedigree of unsurpassed distinction. Two, by including Zengzi and Zisi among the authors of the Four Books, Zhu constructs a direct and unbroken line of transmission of the Way: from Confucius to Zengzi, one of his two greatest disciples; from Zengzi to Zisi, grandson of the Master himself; and finally from Zisi,

---

30 YL 62.1479–1486.

or one of Zisi's disciples, to Mencius. The Four Books' embodiment of the direct line of transmission of the Way no doubt makes their centrality in the later Confucian tradition all the more compelling.]

CHAPTER 1

1.   What heaven decrees is called "the nature"; to follow the nature is called "the Way"; to cultivate the Way is called "instruction."

[Zhu outlines for his readers in the commentary here the metaphysical context that will enable them to understand not only this passage, but the whole of the brief classic: Heaven endows each of the myriad creatures with both psychophysical stuff and principle. In the case of humans, principle is one with human nature. To accord with human nature, thus, is to accord with the Way. But most people will find according with human nature difficult because their psychophysical stuff, which differs with each individual, almost always obscures the nature. This is where cultivation comes in.

These comments reiterate commentarial remarks found in each of the other Four Books, the effect of which is to link the four texts and make a case for their natural coherence.]

2.   The Way: it must not be abandoned for even a moment. What can be abandoned is not the Way. Consequently, the superior man treats with extreme care even that not visible to him; and treats with apprehension even that beyond the reach of his hearing.

[The commentary begins as follows: "The Way is the principle of everyday affairs and things as they ought to be." It goes on to say that the mind-and-heart of the superior man must be ever vigilant and attentive in all matters, even those unseen and unheard; this must be done in order to preserve the heavenly principle that is one with his original nature.]

3.   Nothing is more manifest than the hidden, nothing more obvious than the subtle. Thus the superior man, even in solitude, is watchful over himself.

[The purpose is to keep a check on human desires. According to Zhu, the "hidden" in the text here is speaking of the "subtle, incipient tendencies" of things; these tendencies are active even before things themselves become manifest. The superior man is one who is attentive to and capable of sensing these tendencies and, as a consequence, can gauge matters and things appropriately, responding as he should. For this reason, he can "prevent human desire from germinating" and becoming an obstacle to the realization of his inherent goodness. Whereas the small man, by implication, tends to become the victim of desire, the superior man, by recognizing the stirrings of desire at the onset, is capable of regulating them.]

4. Before pleasure, anger, sorrow, and joy have arisen—this we call perfect balance. After they have arisen and attained due proportion—this we call harmony. Perfect balance is the great foundation of the universe; harmony is the Way that unfolds throughout the universe.

[The commentary remarks that the state before emotions arise refers to human nature alone; and, since human nature is always good, always in accord with rightness, it is a state of perfect moral balance (*zhong*). When emotions are aroused, but in perfect measure, without excess or imbalance, a state of harmony (*he* 和) is achieved. Emotions, then, appropriately expressed, do not becloud the original nature, preventing its actualization as goodness in practice. The great foundation is to be understood as human nature, whereas the Way that penetrates the universe is to be understood as an expression for "following human nature." The great foundation is the "substance" of the Way, the Way as it normatively is; the Way that unfolds is the "function" of the Way, that is, the Way in actual operation.

This passage should make clear that Neo-Confucians do not find emotions themselves problematic; it is excessive or imbalanced emotions that concern them.]

5. Let perfect balance and harmony be realized and heaven and earth will find their proper places therein; and, the ten thousand creatures will be nourished therein.

[Such is the influence of the superior man who himself has achieved perfect moral balance and harmony. The commentary explains, "Now, heaven, earth, and the ten thousand creatures form one body with us. If our mind-and-heart is set in the right, the mind-and-heart of heaven and earth likewise will be set in the right. If our psychophysical stuff is in good order, the psychophysical stuff of heaven and earth likewise will be in good order." The interrelatedness of the cosmos is underscored by Zhu here. It is this interrelatedness that accounts for the power of the sage, in his perfection, to bring order and fulfillment to the universe and all things in it.

Zhu Xi offers the following remark at the conclusion to Chapter 1 of *Maintaining Perfect Balance*. Like his introduction to the text, this paragraph has been treated as part of the classic itself by the later tradition:]

In this, the first chapter, Zisi transmits the ideas handed down by the Confucian school; it is this that is the basis of his discussion. First, he makes clear that the source of the Way is to be found in heaven and is unchangeable, and that its substance, being complete within us, must not be abandoned. Next, he speaks of the essentials of preserving and cultivating it [the mind-and-heart] and examining within oneself. Last, he speaks of the merits and moral influence of sages and spiritual persons. It seems that, in these matters, he wants students to turn and inquire within in order to get it for themselves—and so eliminate the selfishness aroused by external temptations and bring to fulfillment their original goodness. This is what Yang [Shi][31] meant when he said, "Herein lies the gist of the entire work. In the next ten chapters, Zisi, it seems, cites the words of the Master to complete the meaning of this chapter."

[Zisi transmits in this first chapter a holistic cosmic vision where heaven, human beings, and the sociopolitical order are inextricably linked. The Way has its origins in heaven; human beings are to nurture this Way, the substance of which is endowed in each of us; sages and spiritual persons, through the outward manifestation of this Way, effect perfect

---

31 Yang Shi (1053–1135) was a prominent disciple of Cheng Yi and an influential thinker in his own right.

harmony among heaven, earth, and the ten thousand creatures. That is, the Way of heaven and the Way of human beings become one through the agency of sages and spiritual persons.]

CHAPTER 2

1.   Zhongni (Confucius) said, "The superior man maintains perfect balance and keeps to the constant; the small man turns his back on perfect balance and the constant."

2.   The superior man maintains perfect balance and keeps to the constant because, as a superior man, he accords with circumstances in finding the perfect balance. The small man turns his back on perfect balance and the constant because, as a small man, he is devoid of fear and restraint.

[Preserving the balance is situational and is determined by the circumstances of the moment. There is no unchanging, absolute standard of right. The challenge for the individual is to weigh all circumstances sensitively and behave in a manner fully appropriate to those circumstances.

Most translators and commentators understand the *shi* of *shi zhong* 時中 to mean "at all times," understanding *shi zhong* to mean "to practice the mean constantly." This is a legitimate reading. But Zhu wants to emphasize the "situationality" in the practice of preserving the balance. Thus he comments, "It would seem that there is no fixed shape to the preservation of perfect balance; it depends on the circumstances of the moment." (*sui shi* 隨時; lit., "accords with the times")]

CHAPTER 3

The Master said, "Maintaining perfect balance and holding to the constant: this is the highest attainment. For a long time now few people have shown the capacity for it."

[The commentary claims that in the beginning all people shared this capacity and thus keeping perfect balance and holding to the constant was not especially difficult. Over time, however, moral teachings have declined and, consequently, the people have not been roused to maintain perfect moral balance.]

CHAPTER 6

The Master said, "Shun! Great indeed was his knowledge! Shun loved to question others and loved to examine even simple speech. The bad he would keep concealed; the good he would proclaim widely. From among the good he would take hold of the two ends and employ the perfect balance in dealing with the people. This is what made him Shun."

[The commentary remarks: One way to arrive at the mean is to call upon the advice of good men and, with deliberation, sort out the good from the bad; then, reflecting on the good advice, to determine the most appropriate course of action to take under the circumstances.]

CHAPTER 7

The Master said, "People all say, 'I know.' But drive them into a net, a trap, or a pit, and none will know how to escape. People all say, 'I know,' but having chosen to maintain perfect balance and to hold to the constant, they are unable to abide by them for even a month."

[People may know that misfortune has befallen them but do not know how to escape: is this real knowing? They may be able to choose the proper course, but if they cannot hold to it, is this real knowing?]

CHAPTER 8

The Master said, "Here is what [Yan] Hui was like as a person: having chosen to maintain perfect balance and to hold to the constant, when he got hold of a good thing, he would clutch it to his breast and never let it go."

[Hui is contrasted here to the ordinary people referred to in the previous passage.]

Chapter 9

The Master said, "Empire, state, and family can be well governed; rank and salary can be renounced; swords with naked blades can be trampled on. But as for maintaining perfect balance and holding to the constant, it cannot be done."

[The first three matters seem difficult, but for those with the right disposition and the willingness to work hard they are easy. Maintaining perfect balance and the constant may seem easy, but for most people, in the end, it is impossible. It requires that a person be fierce in his pursuit of true goodness and free of even the slightest selfish desire. This is why "few people have shown the capacity for it" (See ch. 3, p. 113).]

Chapter 11

1. The Master said, "To inquire into the obscure and to practice the eccentric so as to gain renown among later generations: this I simply would not do."

[This speaks of "overshooting," for cynical purposes no less. The superior man seeks to maintain what is the perfect balance in the particular circumstances, choosing to practice only the good.]

2. For the superior man to conduct himself in accord with the Way but to give it up midstream—I, for one, would be incapable of stopping.

[This is a reference to the superior man who, of course, knows he should persist but cannot summon up the strength in practice. This is "to fall short."]

3. For the superior man to entrust himself to perfect balance and the constant, and to withdraw from the world unrecognized without any regrets—no one but a sage is capable of this.

[The superior man cares not about "inquiring into the obscure" and "practicing the eccentric," but only about achieving perfect balance and the constant; winning worldly recognition is of no concern to him. And he simply is incapable of giving up midway. Such a person is a sage.

Zhu here reminds the reader of what he said at the end of Chapter 1, that with this chapter Zisi brings to a close the portion of the text in which he cites the words of the Master as an elucidation of the opening chapter. Zhu, in arranging the text and in ascribing authorship as he does, in his view is making explicit the natural coherence and organization of the text—and of the Four Books as a collection.]

Chapter 13

1.   The Master said, "The Way is not far from man. If a person in following the Way distances himself from other men, it cannot be considered the Way."

2.   The *Book of Odes* says:

"Hew an axe handle, hew an axe handle;
The model is near at hand." [#158]

We take hold of one axe handle in order to hew another axe handle. Yet if we look from one to the other, the two appear far different. Therefore, the superior man uses the Way of man to govern men. When they are reformed, he stops.

[This passage has posed problems for commentators and translators alike. The character *gu* 故 ("Therefore") indicates a consequential relationship between "the superior man uses the Way of man to govern men" and the lines that precede it. But why "the superior man uses the Way of man to govern men" as a consequence of finding one axe handle far different from the other has been a source of puzzlement and disagreement among commentators. Indeed, it is possible that the text here is corrupt or that a line or two before the "therefore" has been lost.

Zhu Xi, in his attempt to make sense of the passage, explains that although the axe-handle wielded by the carver may, owing to its proximity, serve as a model for the carved axe-handle, there cannot but be differences between the two, especially in the eyes of the carver himself. Knowing this, when the superior man governs men, he takes as his model that which already inheres in each and every man: the Way of being human, that is, the innate good nature. As Zhu reads this passage then, the model for the axe handle may be close at hand, but because it is external it can never be realized perfectly. By contrast, because the model for being perfectly human is internal to man, it can readily be fully realized by all men through the guidance and example of the superior man. Once men have perfected themselves and become model human beings, there is no need for the superior man to govern.]

3.   Being true to himself and empathetic toward others he keeps near to the Way.[32] What he does not wish done to him he does not do unto others.[33]

[The superior man looks within and first takes measure of his own feelings in gauging the feelings of others. Hence, "the model for an axe handle is near at hand." If he gauges the feelings and needs of others, whatever the circumstances, he is sure to treat those others as the circumstances require. In turn, this behavior serves as a template for others, giving similar shape to their behavior. Hence, "We take hold of one axe handle in order to hew another axe handle." This passage echoes major themes found in the text of the *Analects*.]

4.   The Way of the superior man involves four things, and I, Qiu (Confucius), have so far been incapable of any of them. In serving my father, I have been incapable of doing what is expected of a son; in serving my prince, I have been incapable of doing what is expected of a minister; in serving my older brother, I have been incapable of doing what is expected of a younger brother; in reaching out to friends, I have been incapable of doing what is expected of a friend. Now take the practice of everyday virtue and the exercise of care in everyday speech: if it [virtue] is inadequate he [the superior man] dares not but exert himself; if it [speech] is excessive he dares not but exercise reserve. His speech looks to his practice, and his

---

[32] See *Analects* #19.
[33] Ibid., #94.

practice looks to his speech. Is he, the superior man, not deeply sincere!

[Confucius here is setting up an ideal and—modestly—contrasting his behavior to that of the truly superior man. This passage takes us back to the concept of perfect balance: the actions of a superior man ultimately depend on his keen judgment of what is appropriate in each given set of circumstances; taking measure of his own self enables him to make the right judgment.]

CHAPTER 14

1.   The Master said, "The superior man does what is proper to the station in which he finds himself. He has no desire to go beyond. In a position of wealth and high status he does what is proper to a position of wealth and high status; in a position of poverty and low status he does what is proper to a position of poverty and low status; in a position among barbarians he does what is proper to a position among barbarians; in a position of misfortune and hardship he does what is proper to a position of misfortune and hardship. The superior man never finds himself in a place where he is uncomfortable."

2.   In a superior position he does not offend subordinates; in a subordinate position he does not lean on superiors. He corrects himself and demands nothing from others and thus feels no ill will. Above he feels no ill will toward heaven; below he bears no grudge against men.

3.   For this reason, the superior man lives at ease awaiting his fate. The small man takes dangerous paths seeking undeserved fortune.

[Fortune and prosperity are not within the control of man; they are fated. Thus seeking them is of no use. This is an echo of #40 of the *Mencius*.]

4. The Master said, "The archer in some ways is similar to the superior man. Upon missing the target they turn their gaze inward and seek the cause within themselves."

[Society is—and should be—hierarchical, according to Confucian doctrine. We all find ourselves in different relational settings at different times. These different settings require different behavior, if social order is to be maintained. It is by looking within that the good man knows how to behave relationally, how to maintain the normative hierarchy. Preservation of the social order thus depends upon perfection of the self.]

CHAPTER 20

1. Duke Ai asked about governing.

2. The Master said, "The government under Wen and Wu is displayed on wooden tablets and bamboo slips. When the [right] people are retained, government flourishes; when they are not, government decays."

3. "Such men follow a course that leads to the rapid development of government just as earth follows a course that leads to the rapid growth of vegetation. This government is like easy-growing reeds and rushes."

4. "Thus, governing rests with men. Men are obtained by means of the ruler's own person; his person is cultivated by pursuit of the Way; and the Way is cultivated through the practice of true goodness."

5. "True goodness is what it means to be human; to be loving toward kinfolk is what is important here. Righteousness is to accord with right; to respect the worthy is what is important here. The different grades of love for relatives and the varying degrees of respect for the worthy are given life by ritual."

7. "Thus the superior cannot but cultivate his person; in longing to cultivate his person, he cannot but serve his relatives; in longing to serve his relatives, he cannot but know men; and, in longing to know men, he cannot but know heaven."

8. "The universal Way of the world is fivefold, and the means of putting it into practice are three. Ruler and minister, father and son, husband and wife, elder brother and younger brother, and friend and friend: these five relationships constitute the universal Way of the world. Wisdom, goodness, and courage: these three are the universal virtues of the world. The means of putting them into practice is oneness."

[By "oneness" here is meant "truthfulness," according to Zhu. Cheng Yi earlier, in conversation with his disciples, had commented, "Oneness is what is meant by truthfulness,"[34] explaining that to be *cheng* 誠 ("true"), a person has to keep his original mind unified, free from deception and creaturely desire. It is Cheng's understanding that Zhu Xi brings to his reading of the last line here.]

9. "Some are born knowing it [the universal Way of the world]; others know it through study; and still others know it only through painful effort. But in knowing it they are the same. Some practice it with ease; others practice it with an eye to the benefits it will bring; and still others force themselves to practice it. But in their achievement of it, they are the same."

10. The Master said, "To love learning is to get close to knowing it; to practice it with all one's strength is to get close to true goodness; to know shame is to get close to courage."

11. "Knowing these three things is to know how to cultivate oneself; knowing how to cultivate oneself is to know how to govern others; knowing how to govern others is to know how to govern the empire, the state, and the family."

---

34 *Henan Chengshi yishu*, p. 346.

[Cultivation of the self as the basis of order and harmony in the family, the state, and the empire is the theme of the *Great Learning;* see especially #4–5.]

12. "All in all, in governing empire, state, and family, there are nine canons of conduct: cultivating the self; honoring the worthy; showing affection toward relatives; reverencing the great ministers; empathizing with the body of officials; treating the common people with parental love; giving encouragement to the hundred artisans; dealing gently with travelers from afar; and embracing the lords of all the states."

15. "All in all, in governing empire, state, and family, there are nine canons of conduct. The means of putting them into practice is oneness."

17. "If those in subordinate positions do not gain the confidence of their superiors, they cannot govern the people well. There is a way to gain the confidence of one's superiors: he who is not trusted by friends will not gain the confidence of his superiors. There is a way to win the trust of one's friends: he who is not obedient to his parents will not win the trust of his friends. There is a way to be obedient to one's parents: he who turns inward and finds that he is not true to himself will not be obedient to his parents. There is a way to make oneself true: he who does not understand perfect goodness will not be true to himself."

[The sequence here is familiar: first, perfecting the self; next, bringing order and harmony to the family and community; and, finally, governing the empire well.]

18. "To be true is the Way of heaven. To make oneself true is the Way of man. He who *is* true [i.e., whose virtue is naturally in accord with heavenly principle] maintains perfect balance without effort and apprehends without thinking; he is centered naturally and comfortably in the Way. Such is the sage! He who *makes* himself true chooses the good and holds to it firmly."

19.   "Study it widely, inquire into it thoroughly, ponder it carefully, sift it clearly, practice it diligently."

20.   "Some things he [the superior man] may not study; when he does study he does not desist until he understands it. Some things he may not inquire about; when he does inquire he does not desist until he knows the answer. Some things he may not ponder; when he does ponder he does not desist until he gets it. Some things he may not sift; when he does sift he does not desist until he is clear. Some things he may not practice; when he does practice he does not desist until his practice is diligent. What a person can do in one try, he will dedicate a hundred tries to; what a person can do in ten tries, he will dedicate a thousand tries to."

21.   "If truly capable of pursuing this path, even the dullard is certain to gain clear understanding, and even the weak is certain to grow strong."

[The passage begins with the observation that good government depends on good men, and that attracting good men depends upon the ruler manifesting his goodness. Much of the rest of the passage speaks to the issue of how the ruler manifests goodness—beginning with the cultivation of self.

Paragraph 8 introduces the five normative relations of Confucian teachings: ruler/minister, father/son, husband/wife, older brother/younger brother, and friend/friend. When these relations are fully harmonious, the hierarchy of society is well ordered; when the hierarchy of society is as it should be, the Way can prevail throughout the empire. The "five relations" become a shorthand in the Chinese tradition for all human relations, including those between elder and younger and between male and female. In the commentary on this paragraph Zhu remarks that the three universal virtues of the world refer simply to heavenly principle, which of course is received by all of us from heaven. But to realize the three in practice we must keep ourselves true (*cheng*). To be true is to be true to our endowment of human nature, to the virtues embodied therein; the implication, of course, is that being true to our human nature, we are sure to be true to heaven and to all of those with whom we come into contact.

The ordinary person is different from the sage, whose being in every respect is one with heavenly principle. For him, *being* true is effortless; no process of becoming true is necessary. Most of us, however, have to exert ourselves *to become* true. For, whereas we are all born with the same human nature, which is in every instance good, we are also born with individuated endowments of psychophysical stuff. This of course explains why some people are dullards and some people are weak. But with effort—especially studying and learning—we can all transform our particular endowment of the stuff and return to what it means to be truly human. It is this, according to the commentary, that is the process of becoming true.

Cheng, a term central to *Maintaining Perfect Balance*, has frequently been translated as "sincerity" or "to be sincere." Although not without some merit, "sincerity," in my view, is inadequate. To be sincere implies for many, primarily, a feeling or emotion of genuineness projected outwardly, toward something, that is, to be sincere toward others. To these readers, only secondarily—if at all—does it convey the sense of first being genuine to ourselves. For Zhu and the later Chinese, *cheng* is foremost the process and capacity of being true to ourselves, of being true to the human nature endowed in us. And, by being true to ourselves, we naturally are true toward others in our dealings with them. In short, "to make oneself true" conveys the inner dimension of *cheng* more effectively than "to make oneself sincere."]

CHAPTER 21

When understanding proceeds from truthfulness, this can be attributed to human nature. When truthfulness proceeds from understanding, this can be attributed to instruction. Being true, one understands; understanding, one can arrive at truthfulness.

[This passage is linked by the commentary to Chapter 20, paragraph 18. Though the end result is the same, being true and becoming true represent distinctive approaches to truthfulness (*cheng*). Being true refers to the effortlessness of the sage, who because of the purity of his psychophysical stuff realizes perfection or truthfulness—and consequently genuine understanding—without conscious activity. Becoming true refers to the effort of refining the stuff, that is, of learning the good and holding on to it. This is the self-cultivation of the worthy. The sage, in the view of the commentary, accords with the Way of heaven, whereas the worthy accords with the Way of man. It is this distinction that Zhu brings to his reading of the last line (a rather forced reading, given the syntax of the line), which tries to suggest that for most of us there is a gap, an additional effort required, between the process of learning and the goal of becoming true.]

CHAPTER 22

Only he who is most perfectly truthful[35] is able to give full realization to his human nature; able to give full realization to his human nature, he is then able to give full realization to the human nature of others; able to give full realization to the human nature of others, he is then able to give full realization to the nature of other creatures; able to give full realization to the nature of other creatures, he can then assist in the transformative and nourishing processes of heaven and earth. If he can assist in the transformative and nourishing processes of heaven and earth, he can then form a trinity with heaven and earth.

[This is a reflection of the cosmic vision of *Maintaining Perfect Balance*. The principle of human nature is one with the principle of all things in the universe, including heaven and earth themselves. Through the realization of this principle an individual can understand all things in the world and thus help them to come to realize their inner, natural capacities. This is where his power of transforming and nourishing comes in; this is where the sage, "he who is most perfectly truthful," becomes a partner with heaven and earth.

A major theme in the *Analects*, of course, is the power, the moral power, that the superior man exercises on those around him. This

---

35 *Tianxia zhicheng* 天下至誠, lit., "the most perfectly truthful in the world," is glossed by Zhu as "the fruits of the sage's virtue, to which the world can add nothing." Hence, my translation: "most perfectly truthful," to which nothing can be added.

passage expands on that theme, as is it understood by Zhu Xi. For him this paragraph refers to the metaphysical grounds on which his transformative powers over others—humans and creatures alike—rest. And with this paragraph the status of the sage is elevated to that of the primal generative powers of the universe, heaven and earth. The enormity of the sage's potency is revealed in this passage.]

CHAPTER 23

Next is he who cultivates the shoots of goodness. The shoots being cultivated he is able to attain to truthfulness.[36] Truthfulness then takes on form; with form it becomes apparent; apparent, it becomes bright; bright, it moves others; moving others, it changes them; changing them, it brings about their transformation. Only he who is most perfectly truthful is able to bring about transformation.

[This speaks of the worthy and those below, in contrast to the sage. The worthy man must actively cultivate himself, bringing the germs of goodness, with which he is born (as Mencius argues), to full realization. Note that once the individual has undergone the self-cultivation process, his effect on those around him is the same as that of the sage.]

CHAPTER 25

1.   With truthfulness comes self-completion; with the Way comes guidance.

2.   Truthfulness is the beginning and end of things; without truthfulness there is nothing. It is for this reason that the superior man places great value on truthfulness.

[In conversations with disciples Zhu illustrates what is meant, explaining that if a person is not entirely true in his filiality it is not really filiality; if he is not entirely true in his fraternal respect it is not really

---

36 Zhu explains the character *qu* 曲 (lit., "part, bend, corner") in this line as "germs or shoots of goodness."

fraternal respect.[37] The concept of truthfulness thus relates to the Confucian ideal of the rectification of names, of keeping words and reality in accord.]

3.   Truthfulness is not merely the completion of self and nothing more; by means of it other things become complete. Completion of the self is true goodness; completion of other things is wisdom. These are virtues belonging to human nature; these are the Way that unites external and internal. Thus, employ them according to circumstances and things will be as they should.

[Zhu remarks that true goodness and wisdom are virtues belonging to man's inborn nature. Having brought the self to fulfillment through truthfulness, the superior man achieves inner moral perfection. This inner moral perfection in turn manifests itself in the perfectly humane treatment of those things in the world with which he interacts. Such treatment cannot but have a powerfully transforming effect on those things.

Drawing on traditional dyadic terminology, Zhu equates true goodness here with the preservation of "substance" (*ti*) and wisdom with the issuing forth of "function" (*yong*).]

CHAPTER 26

1.   For this reason perfect truthfulness takes no rest.

2.   Taking no rest, it endures; being enduring, it becomes manifest.

3.   Manifest, it reaches far; reaching far, it expands everywhere; expanding everywhere, it is lofty and bright.

4.   It is because it is expansive that it envelops all things. It is because it is lofty and bright that it shelters all things. It is because it is enduring and far-reaching that it completes all things.

---

37 YL 64.1580.

5. In its expansiveness, it is the coequal of earth; in its loftiness and brightness, it is the coequal of heaven. Far-reaching and enduring, it has no boundaries.

6. This being its nature, it becomes manifest though it makes no display; it effects change though it is unmoving; it brings about completion though it takes no action.

7. The Way of heaven and earth can be perfectly expressed in one word [truthfulness]. This thing [the Way] is without doubleness; its production of all things is thereby unfathomable.

8. The Way of heaven and earth is broad; it is deep; it is lofty; it is bright; it is far-reaching; and it is enduring.

[Truthfulness is the link between heaven, man, and earth. As for heaven and earth, they are by nature true to themselves at all times; but man, because of his endowment of psychophysical stuff, in most cases must dedicate himself to a cultivation process that enables truthfulness to manifest itself. By becoming true, he shares in the nature of heaven and earth (as their principle is one); thus, he has the same power to transform and nourish human beings and the other myriad creatures as do heaven and earth. The extraordinary cosmic power and influence of the perfected man is no better expressed in the canon than here.]

CHAPTER 27

1. Great indeed is the Way of the sage!

2. Overflowing, it produces and nourishes the ten thousand things; in its greatness it extends all the way to heaven.

3. How abundantly great: there are three hundred general rules of propriety and three thousand lesser rules of conduct.

4. Only with the right person can it be followed.

5.   Thus it is said, "Unless there be perfect virtue, the perfect Way does not materialize."

6.   Therefore, the superior man honors his inborn virtuous nature, and follows the path of inquiry and learning. He achieves breadth and greatness, and attends exhaustively to the minute and subtle. He reaches the heights of the lofty and bright, and pursues the course of perfect balance and the constant. He reviews the old, and comes to know the new. Dedicated to kindliness, he esteems the practice of ritual.

[In this paragraph the superior man is distinguished from the sage and is advised on how to achieve the Way of the sage, which is the subject of the previous five paragraphs.]

7.   For this reason, when occupying a position of superiority, he is not overbearing; as a subordinate, he is not disobedient. When the Way prevails in the kingdom, his words enable him to rise to official position; when the Way does not prevail, his silence enables him to endure. The *Book of Odes* says, "Intelligent and wise too, he protects his person." [#260]

[Zhu remarks in the commentary that honoring the moral nature is the means of holding on to the original mind-and-heart and that following the path of inquiry is the means of extending knowledge to the utmost (as prescribed in the *Great Learning*). In his words, "These are the two great seeds of cultivating virtue and consolidating the Way."

Drawing further on the metaphysical language of the day, he goes on to say that crucial to honoring the moral nature and holding on to the original mind-and-heart is ridding oneself of all the selfish desires associated with an imbalanced endowment of psychophysical stuff. He also writes that crucial to honoring the moral nature and extending knowledge to the utmost is the apprehension of the principle of things through investigation.

Although ritual does not receive the sustained attention in *Maintaining Perfect Balance* that it does in the *Analects*, this chapter reminds the reader of its centrality in Confucian social conduct, suggesting that humane and compassionate behavior toward others results naturally from perfection of the self, taking expression in ritual practice.]

CHAPTER 32

1.   Only he who is most perfectly truthful is able to put in order the world's great invariable human relations, to establish the world's great foundation, and to know the transformative and nourishing processes of heaven and earth. Need he depend on anything else?

2.   Earnest and sincere, he is true goodness! Quiet and deep, he is the fountainhead! Vast and great, he is heaven!

3.   Who but one truly quick of apprehension, possessed of sagely wisdom, and with a penetrating understanding of heavenly virtue is able to know him?

[This chapter emphasizes the cosmic greatness of the sage. Being perfectly true—to himself, to others, to heaven, and to earth—he serves as a model for his and later generations; human relations thereby conform to the ideal. The great foundation here is a reference to the substance of human nature; through his realization of human nature he establishes the basis for a social and cosmic order in which not the slightest falsity is present. The commentary on paragraph 3 concludes with the remark that "it is a sage alone who is able to know a sage."

This text, *Maintaining Perfect Balance,* is a sort of rhapsody on the greatness of the sage, describing the supreme virtues and powers of the man who, by perfecting himself, becomes the moral axis of the cosmos. As the text that brings to ultimate conclusion the program of self-cultivation introduced in the *Great Learning,* the *Analects,* and the *Mencius,* Zhu Xi placed it last among the Four Books in his prescribed sequence of reading.]

CONCLUSION

INTERPRETING THE FOUR BOOKS

Since these Four Books were the core curriculum of a Chinese education in the late imperial period, we need to consider what the diligent Chinese student who had dedicated a good decade or so to reading them, reciting them over and over, memorizing them word for word, and fully savoring their flavor might have learned from them. What message had he heard? What teachings had he encountered? What values and ideals had he found?

The Four Books set forth in detail the model characteristics of good behavior: being filial toward your parents; showing respect toward your elders; being true and loyal to others; caring for the young and the aged; treating others empathetically; being true to yourself; not glossing over your mistakes; being humble; not being selfish or egotistical; and not being guided by profit. The list could go on.

But characterizing the constituents of good behavior is only a small part of what truly interests the authors of the Four Books. Their more abiding concern is in examining *how* it is that a person can act morally, that is, what enables a person to become a good human being. Where does his capacity for fully moral behavior lie? It is this concern, more than the elaboration of characteristics of good behavior, that drew thinkers like Zhu Xi to the texts. By taking up matters such as human nature, the mind-and-heart, desires and emotions, learning, and the investigation of things, the Four Books, in the view of Zhu Xi and the Neo-Confucian tradition, provide a compelling explanation of man's moral condition and moral potential.

According to the Four Books, the basis of human morality is to be found in the nature of man. Each and every human being is endowed by heaven at birth with a nature that is good; the challenge every person faces is to give realization to that goodness, to fulfill his heavenly endowed potential. It is the process of self-cultivation described in the Four Books that offers to every individual the means of achieving moral perfection. These coupled assumptions— that all people have the same good human nature and that every person is thus morally perfectible—constitute the philosophical foundation on which the teachings of the Four Books rest. "All people can become a Yao or Shun" (*Mencius*, passage #38).

The matter of human nature is addressed throughout the Four Books, but its treatment is most vivid and emphatic in the *Mencius*. Human beings, Mencius claims, are naturally inclined to be good just as water is naturally inclined to flow downhill (*Mencius* #29). This is a point he elaborates on at length and with frequency: what in particular makes human nature good, he argues, is that it contains the seeds or beginnings of the cardinal virtues of true goodness, righteousness, propriety, and wisdom. Although people, of course, cannot see or touch the four seeds, these seeds nonetheless are every bit as essential to what it means to be human as having the four limbs. How can we know this is the case? Well, would we not, for example, every one of us, *instinctively* feel compassion on seeing a young, helpless child teetering on the edge of an abyss of a well? That this feeling is triggered in each of us, instantaneously and without the slightest deliberation, is sure evidence for Mencius that compassion is something innate to all human beings (*Mencius* #8).

It is crucial to recognize, however, that nowhere in this discussion of the child and the well does Mencius suggest that every one of us, seeing the child at the well's edge, runs to the child's rescue. This is not a lapse or oversight on Mencius' part. For him, the goodness that is human nature is not always realized in practice. Seeing the child's possible fate, all human beings are certain to be filled with alarm and feelings of compassion—but not all rush to the rescue. For, in the moments that follow, some people pause to ask themselves: What will become of me in the attempt to save the child? What if I fail? Will I be held responsible in any way for the child's death? Will I possibly meet with harm or even death as well? What will become of my family should something happen to me?

That is, personal or selfish considerations can readily come between the instinctive response to the child's predicament and the taking of appropriate action.

In this passage and similar ones, Mencius raises the two philosophical issues that, more than any others, will preoccupy Zhu Xi in the twelfth century: (1) If human beings are born good, what accounts for the obvious fact that people do not always manifest goodness in their behavior? and (2) Since the goodness that is human nature is often not manifest, what can and should an individual do to give realization to it? Zhu's lifelong reflection on the canonical tradition was infused with the hope of uncovering how the sages would propose resolving these particular matters. Indeed, it is these concerns that animate much of Zhu Xi's reading of the Four Books and are the ones that his commentarial remarks most eagerly seek to address. In the end, the prominence and distinction that the "learning of the Way" wins in late imperial China owes much to Zhu's compelling and systematic treatment of these issues.

With the *Mencius* as a source of inspiration, Zhu Xi, drawing from the metaphysical language of the day, provides an elaborate philosophical explanation of how there comes to exist a gap between man's innate potentiality for goodness and the expression of that goodness in action. Embracing Mencius' view, he argues that man at birth is endowed by heaven with human nature, and that this human nature is the same in each and every person. It is morally good, constituted, as Mencius had observed, of the four cardinal virtues: benevolence, righteousness, propriety, and wisdom. But—and this is a place where Zhu borrows from contemporary metaphysics to make sense of the canonical tradition—every person is also born with an endowment of *qi* 氣. The quality as well as the quantity of this psychophysical stuff, in contrast to human nature, differ from one individual to another. Some psychophysical stuff is clearer than others, some more refined than others, some lighter and less dense than others. It is this endowment of psychophysical stuff then that accounts for individuation among human beings, giving each person his or her particular form and specific characteristics. And it is this endowment of psychophysical stuff, depending on its degree of clarity and density, that either enables a person's

innately good human nature to shine forth *or* obscures it, thereby
preventing it from becoming manifest.

The particular endowment of stuff that any individual receives
at birth is fated. I happen to receive this quantity and quality of stuff
and you happen to receive that quantity and quality of stuff. But,
importantly, this psychophysical stuff is malleable. The clearest,
most refined stuff, if it is not properly tended to, can become turbid
and coarse, whereas a turbid and coarse endowment can be nurtured
into something more refined and clear. The challenge, for each
human being, is to care for his allotment of psychophysical stuff,
keeping or making it perfectly refined and clear so that the goodness, which is his nature, can reveal itself without obstruction.

Such is the human moral predicament, then, in Zhu's view: Man
lives at all times with the capability of being fully moral and yet
commonly finds himself falling short of moral perfection. He is
presented with an innate moral potential, but one that must actively
and consciously be given realization. To this end, his endowment of
psychophysical stuff has to be nurtured, for it is the condition of his
share of stuff that determines whether his moral potential as a
human being will be achieved.

It is this moral predicament that explains the centrality of the
self-cultivation process in Zhu Xi's philosophical system. Self-
cultivation is the conditioning process, the means by which the individual can refine his psychophysical being, thereby enabling the
goodness that is his human nature to become manifest. This is why,
in Zhu's understanding, the *Great Learning* proclaims, "From the
Son of Heaven on down to commoners, all without exception should
regard self-cultivation as the root" (*Great Learning* #6). That the
text here explicitly calls for every person, irrespective of sociopolitical status, to engage in this cultivation process resonates especially
strongly with Zhu Xi—for if everyone is possessed of the same
moral potential, everyone can become a Yao or Shun.

The ultimate goal of the cultivation process is moral *perfection*,
but rarely is moral perfection achieved. He who achieves it is a sage;
and, according to *Maintaining Perfect Balance*, the power of the sage
is extraordinary, transcending normal human capacity. Like heaven
and earth, the sage—one who has brought himself to the pinnacle

of moral perfection—is possessed of a generative power or force, one that nourishes and transforms all the ten-thousand things in the universe. The sage thus is one who assists heaven and earth in establishing cosmic order (*Maintaining Perfect Balance* ch. 22, ch. 1.5). Straining to put into words the magnificence and wondrous power of the sage, *Maintaining Perfect Balance* describes him as coequal with heaven and earth, and the three together as forming a trinity (*Maintaining Perfect Balance* ch. 22, ch. 26).

How does the aspiring sage realize his moral potential? This is where willpower and effort are essential. Only one filled with the desire and determination to pursue the path toward sagehood can hope someday to achieve it. Few are those who set their mind-and-heart on cultivating the self, who dedicate their efforts to enabling—in the words of the first passage of the *Great Learning*—the "inborn luminous virtue" to shine forth without the slightest obstruction. Fewer still are those who succeed. Confucius, in his famous autobiographical analect, attributes his moral success to a conscious determination, forged at age fifteen, to follow the true Way (*Analects* #8). In the Master's own judgment, it was the fixing of his will on learning the Way of heaven that led him to sagehood. Drawing from the Master's experience and from his reading of the Four Books generally, Zhu Xi attaches great importance to the concept of *lizhi* 立志 ("to fix or establish the will"). In conversations with disciples over decades, he is insistent that any moral progress one hopes to make depends on strengthening the will, that is, on dedicating oneself in mind-and-heart to the program of self-cultivation. In short, the will to improve oneself morally is a prerequisite for moral improvement.

The *Great Learning* does more than exhort people to "regard self-cultivation as the root" (#6). It lays out, step-by-step, a program of self-cultivation (#4–5) that enables an invested individual to nurture and refine his psychophysical endowment and thereby manifest more fully the goodness that is his nature. So important was this program in Zhu Xi's understanding of the Confucian tradition that he gave more than forty years of his life to writing commentary on the brief text of the *Great Learning* and proposed that it be read first among the Four Books, indeed among the entire canon of Thirteen Classics. *Gewu* 格物 ("the investigation of things") was the first and, for Zhu, by far the most critical step in the process of self-perfection. This was the step to which he devoted much of his philosophical attention and the step that the later Neo-Confucian tradition, until the twentieth century, would consider the foundation of moral self-cultivation.

The meaning of *gewu* and of the line in which it appears in the *Great Learning*, *zhihzhi zai gewu* 致知在格物, is by no means transparent, and, in fact, had been understood by earlier commentators and thinkers in a variety of ways. Zhu's reading, influenced strongly by the views of Cheng Yi, the great twelfth-century Neo-Confucian whom he considered his "spiritual master," was different from all earlier readings, colored by the metaphysics that had come of age during the Song. Glossing the character *ge* as *zhi* 至, ("to arrive at or reach"), and the character *wu* as *shih* 事, "thing or affair," he explains the term *gewu* as follows: "to reach to the utmost the principle (*li* 理) in affairs and things with the desire that the extreme point always be reached."

For Zhu, like Cheng Yi before him, everything possesses *li*, conventionally translated as principle. Drawing on remarks by Cheng, Zhu Xi proposes the following summary definition of the term: "With regard to all things in the universe, each and every one of them is certain to have a reason why it is as it is and a rule to which it should conform. This is what is meant by *li* (principle)." Principle thus inheres in each and every thing; and yet, both Cheng and Zhu insist, principle is one. This is the meaning of the often-repeated and well-known formula, "Principle is one, its manifestations are many" (*li yi fen shu* 理一分殊). Whereas each thing, then, is possessed of a particular manifestation of principle, the rule to which all things conform is ultimately one, as is the reason all things are as they are. Perhaps it is best to understand "principle" as something like the underlying pattern or blueprint for the cosmos, a pattern or blueprint that inheres in everything and every affair and in which everything and every affair plays its part. In its ultimate oneness, principle gives coherence and order to the cosmic whole.

It is in Zhu's so-called supplementary chapter to the *Great Learning*, which the later Chinese tradition would treat as part of the body of the classic proper itself, that he provides a clear, summary description of how the investigation of things works and why it is an effective process for moral self-improvement:

> What is meant by "the extension of knowledge lies in the investigation of things" is this: If we wish to extend our knowledge to the utmost, we must probe thoroughly the principle in those things that we encounter. Now every person's intellect is possessed of the capacity for knowing; at the same time every thing in the world is possessed of principle. To the extent that principle is not thoroughly probed a person's knowledge is not fully realized. For this reason, the first step of instruction in the *Great Learning* teaches students that, encountering anything at all in the world, they must build on what they already know of principle and probe still deeper, until they reach its limit. Exerting themselves in this manner for a long time, they will one day suddenly become all-penetrating; this being the case, the manifest and the hidden, the subtle and obvious qualities of all things will all be known and the mind, in its whole substance and vast operations, will be completely illuminated. This is what is meant by "the investigation of things." This is what is meant by "the completion of knowledge."

The process proposed here is an inductive one. Man is required, whenever he encounters any thing, any affair, or any relationship, to look beyond its mere surface. He is to probe into and reflect on the particular manifestation of principle that inheres in it, in order to get at its true thusness. With time and effort, his understanding of things will deepen and broaden, resulting in an ever-clearer apprehension of the world around him. Probing principle thus begins with the particular but yields an understanding of the universal principle that gives coherence to all things. The aim, of course, is not an understanding of the world for understanding's sake, nor is it scientific inquiry that is being proposed. Rather, if a person is genuinely given to understanding the true nature of things and affairs, if he truly recognizes why things, affairs, and relationships are as they are, he will be capable of dealing with those things, affairs, and relationships he encounters in the world in a perfectly appropriate way. Getting at the various manifestations of principle in the end leads to an enlightened understanding of the cosmic order, which, in turn, results in moral awareness of how ideally one is to comport oneself with respect to all things and affairs in that order. Thus *Maintaining Perfect Balance* says of the superior man: "He accords with circumstances in finding the perfect balance" (*Maintaining Perfect Balance* ch. 2.2).

As Zhu Xi's supplementary chapter in the *Great Learning* indicates, principle can be investigated anywhere and in any thing. An individual could access principle by looking at the natural world and its phenomena; at a filial son; at historical events and persons; at personal experiences and relationships. Principle inheres in all things and affairs, after all. But Zhu worried lest such a broad and undefined field of inquiry discourage individuals from seriously taking up the investigation of things. He wished to provide students of the Way with clearer direction. Thus he narrowed the field, suggesting that looking at books, in particular at the Confucian Classics, would be an especially effective means of investigating principle. In his view, because the Classics had been written by the great sages of antiquity—men who themselves had in their own lives come to apprehend principle fully—principle would be clearly and readily manifest in them. There might be other ways to investigate principle, but studying the writings of the sages was simply most efficient. It is in an attempt to make the investigation of principle as efficient as possible for students of the Way that Zhu singled out the Four Books from among the Thirteen Classics, prescribed a precise order in which they were to be studied, and prepared extensive commentarial guidance on them.

Zhu was fond of recalling for his own disciples #83 of the *Analects*, where Confucius laments: "In ancient times, those who learned did so for the sake of themselves; nowadays those who learn do so for the sake of others." His intent was clear: to remind disciples and others of the real aim of classical learning. Whereas study of the canon might, of course, lead incidentally to worldly success—an examination degree and an official post—the genuine purpose of steeping oneself in the Four Books was moral self-improvement through the apprehension of principle. This is why in spite of his demanding regimen of classical learning for disciples, Zhu could tell them on one occasion, "Book learning is a secondary matter for students."[1] His point was simple: Study of the canonical texts is meant to be a means to a moral end. Do not, he was urging, allow it to become a dry, meaningless scholasticism.

To read and embody the Four Books is to come to know principle, and to come to know principle is to cultivate oneself morally. The process of investigating things, then, although projected outwardly, in the end is nothing more than the cultivation of one's inner moral potentiality. That is, through the investigation of things, especially the study of the canon, the seeds of true goodness, righteousness, propriety, and wisdom that constitute human nature can grow and be given fuller, more meaningful expression in one's actions.

The morality that becomes manifest through the process of self-cultivation is "interrelational." "Goodness" is to be good in one's relations with others. The character for "goodness" (*ren* 仁) is pictographically significant in this respect. It consists of two components, one representing a human being (人) and the other meaning "two" (二). The suggestion is that goodness is something that can be manifested only in relation to other persons, in a community of fellow human beings. The ascetic who sits atop a pillar in the Syrian desert for years ridding himself of all taint of evil to become good in the eyes of the Judeo-Christian God does not exist in the Confucian tradition.

To be good in one's relations with others requires that one be sensitive to status distinctions. Father and son, ruler and subject, husband and wife, old and young, and friend and friend, according to Mencius (3A.4), had become the five paradigmatic relationships binding Chinese society together as early as the reign of the legendary Shun. These are the relationships on which the hierarchical, normative sociopolitical order rests. In the words of *Maintaining Perfect Balance*, it is the five relationships that "constitute the universal Way of the world" (ch. 20.8). A good person acts as he should

---

1 YL 10.161.

as a son toward his father; in the next moment, he acts as he should as a young man toward his aged next-door neighbor; and in the following moment, he acts as he should as a husband toward his wife. Each of these relational contexts calls for a different expression of goodness in one's behavior: filial devotion and affection in the first, respect and deference in the next, and guidance and care in the last. This is what is meant when the Master says, in *Maintaining Perfect Balance* (ch. 14.1), "The superior man does what is proper to the station in which he finds himself."

Perhaps because goodness is relationship dependent, Confucius himself, although deeply preoccupied with virtue, never provides a comprehensive definition of it. Nor does he readily describe people of his day, including himself, as men of true goodness. To be sure, he offers in conversations with disciples characterizations and illustrations of *ren* ("goodness"), but little in the way of definitional explanation. The disciples' persistent questioning throughout the *Analects* about whether, in the judgment of the Master, such-and-such is a matter of true goodness or whether so-and-so is a person of true goodness suggests that the disciples themselves are anxious and wish to have a better, more concrete sense of the meaning of this paramount virtue.

Whatever Confucius' reticence in offering a definition, several exchanges between the Master and his disciples, taken together, convey a reasonable understanding of what makes for *ren*. In #19 of the *Analects*, the Master tells his disciples that though his Way may seem complicated there is a unifying thread that runs through it. The disciples, confused, turn to Zengzi for clarification. He explains almost matter-of-factly: "The Way of our Master is being true to oneself and empathetic toward others (*shu*), nothing more." To be a follower of the Way, an individual must work to be true to his nature, giving full realization to those qualities that make him human—goodness, righteousness, propriety, and wisdom. But these qualities must be projected outwardly, becoming manifest in his relations with others. In this passage, Zengzi suggests that it is through the empathetic treatment of people that innate goodness is extended to others. It is the practice of empathy in relations with others that constitutes true goodness.

The great importance the Master attaches to the practice of empathy is reiterated in a later analect:

> Zigong asked, Is there one word that can be practiced for the whole of one's life? The Master said, That would be "empathy" perhaps: what you do not wish yourself do not do unto others. (#94)

Shu 恕 ("empathy") is briefly explained: it is to treat others as one wishes to be treated oneself. This requires that one be keenly sensitive to others and their particular circumstances, that one be able to put oneself in their place and to take a measure of them and how to treat them using one's own feelings as the standard. To practice empathy does not require extraordinary strength (#18), as all people are equally human, endowed with the same nature, and thus capable of inferring from their own selves the wishes and needs of others. What it does require, however, is an unswerving will or determination to extend oneself to others in this manner.

The challenge for the follower of the Way lies in sustaining an empathetic effort in relations with one person after the other, from one moment to the next, day in day out, for a lifetime. The occasional, self-conscious practice of empathy is relatively easy. It is only when the individual reaches the point where the effort becomes effortless, where he *naturally* and selflessly, in all relations with others, wishes for them what he would wish for himself that he approaches true goodness. In #34, the Master states: "Now wishing himself to be established, the truly good person establishes others; and, wishing himself to achieve prominence, he makes others prominent. The ability to draw analogies from what is near at hand can be called the way to true goodness." Zhu's commentary on the final line here sums up matters nicely:

> To draw from what is near is to draw from oneself; it is to take what one desires oneself and analogize it to others, understanding that what they desire is just the same. Afterward, one approaches others extending to them what they desire, which is a matter of empathy [*shu*] and the way to true goodness [*ren*].

Should people in general come to conduct their relations empathetically, the five relationships of Chinese society—father/son, ruler/
subject, husband/wife, older/younger, and friend/friend—will all
find perfect balance and equilibrium and the sociopolitical order
will enjoy peace and harmony.

Essential to the conduct of social relations is the practice of *li* 禮
("ritual"). It is through ritual behavior that human beings express
themselves to others. The conventional translation for *li*, "ritual,"
should not mislead readers. In speaking of *li*, Confucius surely
intends rituals and ceremonies typically associated with "sacred"
occasions: funerals, ancestral celebrations, weddings, and cappings,
which take place when a young man achieves adulthood. But, for
him, ritual governs the everyday as well. How people dress, eat,
speak, greet one another, bow, sit, and so forth, these too are matters
of *li*. A person learns—as ritualized behavior toward others—to pick
up dumplings from the bamboo basket with chopsticks and not his
fingers; to address a teacher respectfully and politely and a close
friend more informally, perhaps even with some intimacy; to eat
only once the elders at the table have begun eating; to walk slowly
behind one's elder; and to refrain from touching in public someone
of the opposite sex. Members of his family, especially his mother,
have taught him these "proper ways" to behave from the moment
he emerged from the womb. The family, after all, is deeply invested
in his successful acculturation, as his behavior ultimately reflects on
the family as whole, on their level of "civilization." Thus, with his
behavior constantly overseen by family, the *li*, over time, become
second nature to him.

Confucius recognizes the power that *li* exercise in daily life,
their ability to provide social order and harmony, upholding
the network of hierarchy and authority, without any apparent
compulsion. This explains why he can decry the use of law and
punishment that is becoming ever more popular in his own day.
Laws and punishments are unnecessary, even harmful (#7, #71). He
recognizes too the ability of *li* to promote in each of us a deeper
sense of humanity, enabling us, individually, to feel meaningfully
connected to others, integrated into a community that transcends
the isolated self.

The Master repeatedly cautions, however, that ritual practice—whether it is paying respect to ancestors before the ancestral tablets, serving the family elders at a meal, bowing before the new village school teacher, sitting only on a mat that is straight (#60), comforting a grieving friend, greeting a neighbor on the street—cannot be mechanical or rote, but must be sustained by genuine feeling. Appreciating the danger that ritualized behavior, through its repetitiveness, can easily give way to empty, merely formal gesture, Confucius insists that it is the feeling behind the practice that gives meaning to ritual. It is this feeling that gives ritual its efficacy. This is why he asks rhetorically in #103, " 'Ritual, ritual': does it mean nothing more than jade and silk?" Ritual practice that is mechanical and hollow, unaccompanied by an inner spirit or feeling, is not authentic ritual practice. It has no affective force, no real power to promote social good and harmony; nor does it provide the performer himself with any uplift, any feeling of humanitarian satisfaction. It is essential then, in his view, that the performance of ritual be infused with the spirit of goodness. In #14, Confucius says, "If he is a man (*ren*) but not truly good (*ren*), what does he have to do with ritual? If he is a man but not truly good, what does he have to do with music?" The Master returns to this point frequently, apparently worried because ritual form can easily become empty of all feeling. Passage #9 of the *Analects* expresses this anxiety especially well: "Ziyou asked about filial piety. The Master said, Nowadays to be 'filial' means simply to be capable of providing parents with nourishment. But even dogs and horses get their nourishment from us. Without the feeling of reverence, what difference is there?" The Master's discussion of ritual throughout the *Analects* is an effort to effect a rectification between name and reality: ritual uninformed by spirit and feeling is not true ritual.

As an overarching authority, the government is especially well placed to promote the moral development of the people; it thus figures prominently in the Four Books. The ideal government, a government that is morally good, does not only advance social and political order, but morally transforms the people as well (#7). By leading with exemplary virtue and ritual sensitivity, the ruler and his government awaken in the people an awareness of their own innate potentiality for virtue and good behavior toward others. A sort of resonance, based on the universality of human nature, thus occurs between the ruler and the people he governs.

The ruler thus must be attentive to the cultivation of his own virtue, for the rectification of those he governs takes its beginning in his person. Thus, when Ji Kangzi asks Confucius about the way to govern, the Master's response is curt and to the point: "To govern (*zheng* 政) means to correct (*zheng* 正). If you lead by correcting yourself, who would dare to remain incorrect?" (#73). Like the well-known remark "One who practices government by virtue may be compared to the North Star: it remains in its place while the multitude of other stars turn toward it" (#6), this statement speaks to the ruler's ability to move people, silently and without compulsion, toward goodness, through an invisible but profound moral force. The moral suasion the ruler exercises, almost magically, over those he governs is a theme that runs throughout the Four Books. In another testy, but powerful response to yet another question from Ji Kangzi, this time about whether it would be of benefit to the promotion of the Way to kill those who do not follow the Way, the Master says, "You are governing; what need is there for killing? If you desire good, the people will be good. The virtue of the superior man is wind; the virtue of the small person is grass. When wind passes over it, the grass is sure to bend" (#74).

The very first passage of the *Mencius* takes up precisely this theme. Mencius, after traveling a great distance, meets with King Hui of Liang, who greets him as follows: "Sir. You've come here with little concern for the thousand *li*. Surely you've brought something that will be of profit to my state?" Mencius, chagrined by the question, rebukes the king: "Why must Your Majesty use the word 'profit'? Surely, it is true goodness and righteousness alone that matter" (*Mencius* #1). In a later chapter, Mencius writes, "When the sovereign is truly good, everybody will be truly good; when the sovereign is righteous, everybody will be righteous" (*Mencius* #18).

The *Great Learning* offers a template of sorts for the ruler, stating rather programmatically that to bring tranquility to the empire and moral renewal to the people, the ruler must first make manifest his "inborn luminous virtue." To manifest this virtue, the text continues, he must engage in the process of self-cultivation, which, in turn, has its beginnings in the investigation of things (*Great Learning* #1–5). Good government thus rests on the moral condition of the ruler, on the seriousness with which he takes up cultivation of the self.

Good government then, that is, government that is virtuous, relying on moral force and ritual practice, not law, is the political cornerstone of Confucius' vision. But Confucius himself does not go into great detail about what precisely makes for a moral ruler and moral government. It is left to Mencius to fill in the picture. In his exchanges, especially with feudal rulers of the day, Mencius claims generally that the responsibility of good government is to protect and provide for the people, and then he lays out concrete measures the ruler and government should take to achieve these ends. Among them are tax lightly; do not draw on the labor of the people during farming season; charge no duty at border stations; harvest timber prudently; grant each family a plot of one hundred *mu* to farm; and encourage the planting of mulberry trees and the breeding of chickens and pigs (See the *Mencius* #2, #3, #4, #9).[2]

The concern that underlies all of these specific suggestions is the material well-being of the people. Mencius takes the position here— going well beyond what the Master himself articulates—that, whereas moral cultivation is essential to what it means to be human, such cultivation is a luxury for the person whose subsistence needs are not being met. People struggling merely to survive, anxious about food, clothing, and shelter for themselves, their children, and their aging parents and grandparents, "have not the leisure to attend to ritual and righteousness," Mencius argues (#4). His view on this matter is expressed in direct and powerful language:

> To have a constant mind-and-heart without a constant livelihood is something that a gentleman alone is capable of. If the people lack a constant livelihood it follows that they will lack a constant mind-and-heart. And if they lack a constant mind-and-heart, they

---

2 See *Mencius* 2A.5.

will become reckless and depraved and there is nothing they will
not do. (#4)

Looking after the people's material welfare, therefore, is not
incidental to good government; it is the explicit charge of government—to create an environment where the daily needs of the people
are met, an environment in which people are enabled to become
morally good.

This sort of caring government, in turn, is sure to win the alle-
giance and loyalty of the people: "It is impossible in a state where
the elderly wear silk and eat meat, and the black-haired people suffer
from neither hunger nor cold, for the ruler not to be regarded as a
true king" (#4).[3] Conversely, a ruler who in his governance of the
people does not live up to the responsibilities of a good and true
ruler, who does not provide for the needs of his subjects, may find
himself spurned by them. Worse still, Mencius allows, the people
may depose him (#55, #6, #5, #27). With this threat, Mencius
gives the ruler a powerful incentive to be responsive to those he
governs.

The form of government espoused in the Four Books then is a
sort of a benevolent paternalism, in which it is supposed that the
ruler genuinely and deeply cares for his people just as a father does
for his children. Like a father in his family, the ruler determines
what is best for those under his care. He decides, and his subjects
are expected to follow the direction he charts, on the assumption
that he has weighed their interests conscientiously and concluded
what is the most appropriate direction to take. In its ideal form,
paternalistic rule might qualify as a government *for* the people, but
never should it be thought of as a government *by* the people. In
normal matters of government the people are given no voice to
express their will. Good government depends rather on paternalistic
leadership by a good and caring ruler and his officials.

In the view of the Four Books, ideal government rests on a series
of related moral imperatives: it must rule through virtue; it must set

---

3 See *Mencius* 4B.16 and 4A.9 as well.

an example for others through its moral conduct and empathetic treatment of the people; and it must take appropriate measures to ensure the material well-being of those it governs. Government of this sort is certain to lead to political order and social harmony; but, even more, it is certain to transform the people morally. In short, good government makes the people good. It is this aim that sets the political teachings of Confucianism apart from most other political philosophies.

There is a circularity to the teachings expressed in the Four Books. Government must be good so that the people will become good. But good government is possible only when good people agree to serve in it. Thus we return to the first step here: the self-cultivation of the individual. That is, government requires the assistance of men who already have come to realize the goodness that dwells within them. Through self-cultivation, most especially the dedicated study of the Four Books, they have experienced a moral awakening; and, through their virtue and empathetic treatment of the people they govern, they are capable of bringing about a similar awakening in others.

Over the centuries Chinese rulers relied on the civil service examinations to find such men—at least this was the ideal that lay behind the examination system. From 1300 until 1900, examination candidates were required to demonstrate their mastery of the Four Books—the *Great Learning*, the *Analects*, the *Mencius*, and *Maintaining Perfect Balance*—and Zhu Xi's commentary on them. If these Four Books were the tradition's most reliable guides to moral self-realization, as it was thought, then those who through years of memorization and recitation had come to embody their teachings were sure to lead moral lives. And, in leading moral lives, it was hoped that they would inspire others to lead moral lives.

WORKS CITED

Cheng Yi 程頤 and Cheng Hao 程顥. *Henan Chengshi yishu* 河南程氏遺書. In *ErCheng quanshu* 二程全書. Sibu beiyao edition.

Brown, Arthur Judson. *The Chinese Revolution.* (Student Volunteer Movement: New York, 1912).

Cahill, James. *The Restless Landscape: Chinese Painting of the Late Ming Period* (Berkeley: Chinese Art Museum, 1971).

Doolittle, Justus. *Social Life of the Chinese: With Some Account of Their Religious, Governmental, Educational and Business Customs and Opinions.* (New York: Harper & Bros., 1867).

Gardner, Daniel K. "Confucian Commentary and Chinese Intellectual History." *Journal of Asian Studies* 57.2 (May 1998): 397–422.

———. *Learning to Be a Sage: Selections from the "Conversations of Master Chu,"* Arranged Topically. Berkeley: University of California Press, 1990.

———. "Principle and Pedagogy: Chu Hsi and the Four Books." *Harvard Journal of Asiatic Studies* 44.1 (June 1984): 57–81.

———. "Transmitting the Way: Chu Hsi and His Program of Learning." *Harvard Journal of Asiatic Studies* 49.2 (June 1989): 141–172.

———. *Zhu Xi's Reading of the Analects: Canon, Commentary, and the Classical Tradition.* New York: Columbia University Press, 2003.

Lunyu yinde 論語引得. Harvard-Yenching Institute Sinological Index Series, supplement no. 16. Reprint, Taibei: Chinese Materials and Research Aids Service Center, 1966.

Schwartz, Benjamin I. *The World of Thought in Ancient China.* Cambridge, MA: Harvard University Press, 1985.

Zhao Shunsun 趙順孫. *Lunyu zuanshu* 論語纂疏. In *Sishu zuanshu* 四書纂疏. Taibei: Xinxing shuju, 1972.

Zhuanyuan, Ming. edited by Gu Dingchen. (Beijing: Zhongguo Shudian, 1999).

Zhu Xi 朱熹. *Daxue huowen* 大學或問. In *Sishu daquan* 四書大全, edited by Hu Guang 胡廣. Jinan: Shandong youyi shushe, 1989.

———. *Hui'an xiansheng Zhu Wengong wenji* 晦安先生朱文公文集. Sibu congkan edition.

———. *Sishu jangju jizhu.*

———. *Sishu jizhu* 四書集注. Sibu beiyao edition.

———. *Zhuzi yulei* 朱子語類. Edited by Li Jingde 黎靖德. Beijing: Zhonghua shuju, 1986.

Zi, Etienne. *Pratique des examens littéraires* (Shanghai: Imprimerie de la Mission Catholique, 1894).

EARLIER TRANSLATIONS

I have benefited greatly from earlier translations of each of the Four Books, especially the following:

Akatsuka Kiyoshi 赤塚忠. *Daigaku Chûyô* 大學中庸. *Shinshaku kanbun taikei* 新釋漢文大系, vol. 2. Tokyo: Meiji shoin, 1967.

Bloom, Irene. *Mencius.* In *Sources of Chinese Tradition*, vol. 1, 2nd ed., edited by Wm. Theodore de Bary and Irene Bloom. New York: Columbia University Press, 1999.

Brooks, E. Bruce and Brooks, A. Takeo. *The Original Analects: Sayings of Confucius and His Successors.* New York: Columbia University Press, 1998.

Hinton, David, trans. *Mencius.* Washington, D.C.: Counterpoint, 1998.

Hiraoka Takeo 平岡武夫, trans. *Rongo* 論語. *Zenshaku kanbun taikei* 全釋漢文大系, vol. 1. Tokyo: Shûeisha, 1980.

Lau, D. C., trans. *Confucius: The Analects.* Harmondsworth: Penguin, 1979.

———, trans. *Mencius*. Harmondsworth: Penguin, 1970.

Legge, James. *The Chinese Classics*. Rev. edition. 5 vols. Hong Kong: Hong Kong University Press, 1960.

Plaks, Andrew, trans. *Ta Hsueh and Chung Yung*. London; New York: Penguin, 2003.

Shiso shûchû 四書集注. *Shushigaku taikei* 朱熹學大系, vols. 7–8. Tokyo: Meitoku Shuppansha, 1974.

Slingerland, Edward, trans. *Confucius Analects, with Selections from Traditional Commentaries*. Indianapolis: Hackett Publishing, 2003.

Uchino Kumaichirô 內野熊一郎, trans. *Môshi* 孟子. *Shinshaku kanbun taikei* 新釋漢文大系, vol. 4. Tokyo: Meiji Shoin, 1991.

Uno Seiichi 宇野精一, trans. *Môshi* 孟子. *Zenshaku kanbun taikei* 全釋漢文大系, vol. 2. Tokyo: Shûeisha, 1973.

Waley, Arthur, trans. *The Analects of Confucius*. New York: Vintage, 1938.

Yamashita Ryûji 山下龍二, trans. *Daigaku Chûyô* 大學中庸. *Zenshaku kanbun taikei* 全釋漢文大系, vol 3. Tokyo, Shûeisha, 1974.

Yoshida Kenkô 吉天賢抗, trans. *Rongo* 論語. *Shinshaku kanbun taikei* 新釋漢文大系, vol. 1. Tokyo: Meiji shoin, 1991.

SUGGESTED READINGS

de Bary, W^m. Theodore. *Neo-Confucian Orthodoxy and the Learning of the Mind-and-Heart.* New York: Columbia University Press, 1981.

—— and Chaffee, John W., eds. *Neo-Confucian Education: The Formative Stage.* Berkeley: University of California Press, 1989.

Elman, Benjamin. *A Cultural History of Civil Examinations in Late Imperial China.* Berkeley: University of California Press, 2000.

—— and Woodside, Alexander, eds. *Education and Society in Late Imperial China, 1600–1900.* Berkeley: University of California Press, 1994.

Graham, A. C. *Disputers of the Tao: Philosophical Argument in Ancient China.* La Salle: Open Court, 1989.

—— *Two Chinese Philosophers: Ch'eng Ming-tao and Ch'eng Yi-chuan.* London: Lund Humphries, 1958.

Henderson, John B. *Scripture, Canon, and Commentary: A Comparison of Confucian and Western Exegesis.* Princeton: Princeton University Press, 1991.

Miyazaki, Ichisada. *China's Examination Hell.* Translated by Conrad Schirokauer. New Haven. Yale University Press, 1981.

Nylan, Michael. *The Five "Confucian" Classics.* New Haven: Yale University Press, 2001.

GLOSSARY/INDEX OF IMPORTANT NAMES AND TERMS

Analects xiii, xviii, xi, xxiii, xxv, xxx, 9–49, 54, 62, 73, 78, 96, 99, 100, 108, 117, 124, 128–29, 135, 138, 140–41, 143, 147–149, 150

being true to oneself (*zhong*) 13, 19, 26, 31, 55, 117, 131, 140

Bo Yi 伯夷 101, 102

Book of Etiquette xviii

Book of History xviii, 82

Book of Odes xv, 41, 57–58, 72, 74, 89, 116, 128

Book of Rites xviii, xxi

cheng 誠 (to be true, truthfulness). *See* true/truthfulness.

Cheng brothers. *See* Master Cheng.

Cheng Hao 程灝 xix, xxiii, 19, 148

Cheng Yi 程頤 xix, xxiii, 5, 6, 19, 112, 120, 136, 148

Classic of Changes xv

Classic of Filial Piety xix

Confucius 孔夫子, Zhongni 仲尼 (the Master) xviii, xix, xxv, 3, 5, 7, 8, 11, 12, 13–19, 20, 21–29, 30–34, 35–39, 40–42, 45–49, 55–56, 64, 72–74, 78, 89, 90, 93, 96, 100, 109, 112–18, 120, 135, 138, 140–45, 149, 150

dao 道 (the Way). *See* Way.

Daoist 41, 43

Daoxue 道學 (learning or school of the Way) xiv, xxvii, xxix, 19

de 德 (virtue). *See* virtue.

empathy (*shu*) 18, 19, 27, 42, 43, 44, 96, 140, 141

Erya 爾雅 dictionary xviii

Fan Zhongyan 范仲淹 xix, xxii

filial piety (*xiao*) xix, 15

Five Classics (*wujing*) xv, xviii, xix, xxi–xxii, xxiv–xxvi, 103

function (*yong*) 12, 19, 111, 126

Gaozi 告子 62–64, 84–88, 102

gewu 格物 (investigation of things). *See* investigation of things.

Gongduzi 公都子 71, 88, 93

Gongyang 公羊 *Tradition* xviii

Guliang 穀梁 *Tradition* xviii

Great Learning xiii, xxi, xxiii, xiv–xxv, 3–8, 11, 15, 19, 25, 27, 40–41, 53, 76, 102, 109, 121, 128, 129, 134, 135–38, 144, 145, 147

Han Feizi 韓非子 74

Han Yu 韓愈 xxi, 6

harmony 111, 112, 121

he 和 (harmony). *See* harmony.

Hu Yuan 胡瑗 xix

human nature (*xing*) xxiii, 11, 12, 13, 14–15, 17, 19, 24–27, 35, 40, 60, 64–67, 77, 80, 84–89, 94–96, 99, 102, 103, 110, 111, 122–25, 127, 128, 129, 131–34, 135, 139, 140, 141, 144

inactivity (*wuwei*) 42, 43

inborn luminous virtue (*mingde*) 3–6, 19, 102, 135, 144

investigation of things (*gewu*) 5, 7, 8, 12, 41, 131, 136–39, 145

Ji Kangzi 季康子 36–37, 144

junzi 君子 (superior man). *See* superior man.

King Hui of Liang 梁惠王 53–55, 61, 144

King Xuan of Qi 齊宣王 56, 61–62, 83, 84

li 理 (principle). *See* principle.

li 禮 (ritual). *See* ritual.

Li Ao 李翱 6

Liuxia Hui 柳下惠 101, 102

Maintaining Perfect Balance (*zhong/Zhongyong*) vii, xiii, xxi, xxiii, xxv, 34, 98, 105–29, 134, 135, 138–40, 142, 147

mandate of heaven (*tianming*) 75

Master Cheng 19, 21, 25–26, 28, 33, 55, 64–65, 74, 78, 89, 95, 103, 108

Mencius 孟子 vii, xiii, xxi, xxiii, xxv, 20, 51–103, 108, 118, 129, 132–33, 144–47, 149; *See also*, Mencius xviii, xxv, 27, 51–103, 107, 110, 125, 132–133, 139, 144–146

mind-and-heart (*xin*) 14, 15, 17, 21, 22, 33, 41, 44, 55–59, 61–67, 71–72, 79–81, 88–93, 95, 97, 100–102, 103, 107, 110, 112, 128, 131, 135, 145

mingde 明德 (inborn luminous virtue, perfect virtue). *See* inborn luminous virtue.

Mo Di 墨翟 71, 73, 74, 98, 100

normal/constant (*yong*) 107–108, 109, 113, 114, 115, 116, 127, 134

Ouyang Xiu 歐陽修 xix, xxiii

principle (*li*) 5, 7, 8, 15, 21, 23, 25–26, 28–30, 32–34, 39–41, 46, 65, 71, 74, 78, 79, 80, 86, 89, 95, 96, 99–100, 102, 103, 107–10, 121–24, 127–28, 136, 137–39, 148

probe principle (*qiongli*) 15, 21, 137

psychophysical stuff (*qi*) 3, 14, 25, 32, 35, 45–46, 63–65, 79, 80, 86, 89, 92, 110, 112, 123, 127–28, 133–34

qi 氣 (psychophysical stuff)

qiongli 窮理 (probe principle). *See* probe principle.

rectification of names (*zhengming*) 36, 37, 38, 62, 125

ren 仁 (true goodness, truly good). *See* true goodness/truly good.

Rites of Zhou xviii

ritual/rites (*li*) xviii, xxii, 14–17, 23–24, 26–27, 32, 35, 36, 38, 42, 46, 49, 60, 69, 76–78, 81, 101, 102, 119, 128–29, 142–43, 145

self-cultivation (*xiushen*) xxiii, 5–8, 22, 41–42, 76, 120, 122, 124–25, 127, 132, 134–36, 139, 145, 147

Shen Buhai 申不害 74

Shen Nong 神農 69, 71

shu 恕 (empathy, consideration for others, reciprocity). *See* empathy.

Shun 舜 23, 42–43, 73–74, 77, 79–82, 88–89, 94, 102, 114, 132, 134, 139

Sima Guang 司馬光 xix

Spring and Autumn Annals xviii, 72

Su Dongpo 蘇東坡 xix, xxiii

substance (*ti*) 8, 12, 19, 111, 126, 129, 137

superior man (*junzi*) 11–13, 16–17, 19–21, 23, 28, 31, 36–38, 40, 42, 43, 44, 48–49, 57, 77, 79–81, 99–100, 103, 110–13, 115–18, 122, 124–25, 128, 138, 140, 144

ti 體 (substance). *See* substance

tianming 天命 (mandate of heaven). *See* mandate of heaven.

true/truthfulness (*cheng*) 13, 96, 120, 121–24, 125–28, 129

true goodness/truly good (*ren*) 12–13, 14, 16–18, 22–24, 27–30, 31–32, 34–35, 39, 44, 48, 53–55, 57, 59, 61–62, 67, 69, 75, 77, 78–81, 84, 86–92, 95–98, 100, 103, 115, 119, 120, 126, 128, 132, 139–40, 141, 143, 144

virtue (*de*) 3–6, 13–14, 16, 19–20, 27, 31, 37, 38, 42, 46, 56, 75, 83, 99, 102–103, 117, 121, 124, 128, 135

Wang Anshi 王安石 xix, xxii, xxiii

Wang Yangming 王陽明 6

Way (*dao*) xiv, xxiv, xxv, xxix, 3, 4, 8, 12, 15, 19, 20–25, 29, 30–31, 33, 37, 42, 44, 46–48, 63, 69, 72–76, 89, 93–94, 96, 98–100, 102, 107, 109–13, 115–17, 119–23, 125–28, 133, 135, 138, 139–41, 144

will/determination (*zhi*) 15, 18, 25, 27, 28, 29, 30, 44, 48, 63, 64–65, 93–94, 135, 141

wujing 五經 (Five Classics). *See* Five Classics.

wuwei 無為 (inactivity). *See* inactivity.

xiao 孝 (filial piety). *See* filial piety.

Xie Liangzuo 謝良佐 39

xin 心 (mind-and-heart). *See* mind-and-heart.

xing 性 (human nature). *See* human nature.

xiushen 修身 (self-cultivation). *See* self-cultivation.

Xu Xing 許行 69, 70, 71

Xunzi 荀子 14

Yan Hui 顏回 (Yan Yuan 顏淵) 20, 22, 33, 35, 114, 115

Yang Shi 楊時 112

Yang Zhu 楊朱 71, 73, 98

Yao 堯 xviii, 23, 42, 72–74, 81–82, 89, 94, 102, 132, 134

yin/yang 陰陽 91

yong 用 (function). *See* function.

yong 庸 (normal, constant). *See* normal/constant.

Zengzi 曾子 xxv, 3, 7–8, 13, 19, 28, 109, 140

Zhang Zai 張載 xix, xxiii

zhengming 正名 (rectification of names). *See* rectification of names.

zhi 志 (will, determination). *See* will/determination.

zhong 忠 (being true to oneself, doing one's best, giving full expression to oneself). *See* being true to oneself.

zhong 中 (*maintaining perfect balance*). *See* Maintaining Perfect Balance.

Zhongyong 中庸 (*Maintaining Perfect Balance: Keeping to the Way Amidst Change*). *See* maintaining perfect balance.

Zhou Dunyi 周敦頤 xxiii

Zhu Xi 朱熹 ix, xiv, xxii–xxvi–xxix, 3–8, 11–12, 14–17, 19–21, 23–25, 27–28, 31–33, 35, 39–40, 42–43, 47, 49, 55, 61–62, 64–66, 68, 71, 76, 77–80, 83–86, 88, 89–90, 92, 95–97, 98–99, 107–113, 116, 120, 122–26, 128–29, 131, 133–36, 138–39, 141, 147, 148

Zigong 子貢 16, 20, 23, 30, 34–35, 40, 43, 46, 48, 141

Zilu 子路, Jilu 季路, Zhong You 仲由 16, 33, 34, 36–38, 42, 47

Zisi 子思 xxv, 107, 109–10, 112, 116

Zixia 子夏, Shang 商 34, 48

Ziyou 子游 15, 143

Zizhang 子張, Shi 師 34

Zuo 左 *Tradition* xviii